Give Your Heart a Break

A TEDx speaker and marketing consultant settled in Mumbai, **Anuj Tiwari** was brought up on the bustling streets of Bareilly. Tiwari studied in a Hindi-Sanskrit-medium school where there were no English books. Seeing the kids of his neighbourhood reading colourful storybooks, he started building dreams of being able to read in English; however, he kept those dreams to himself.

Despite going through six months of depression and severe anxiety and trying to give up on his life in college, Tiwari is now the bestselling author of four books, inspired by real-life incidents. He has also been listed as one of the top ten most influential authors in India in 2016.

This book is Anuj Tiwari's most personal creation, inspired by his own family.

Instagram: anujtiwariofficial
Facebook: www.facebook.com/anujtiwari.official
Email: anujtiwari.official@gmail.com
Twitter: @AnujOfficial

Other bestsellers by Anuj Tiwari

Journey of Two Hearts!
It Had To Be You
It's Not Right...But It's Okay
I Tagged Her in My Heart

Give Your Heart a Break

ANUJ TIWARI

Published by
Rupa Publications India Pvt. Ltd 2019
7/16, Ansari Road, Daryaganj
New Delhi 110002

Sales Centres:
Allahabad Bengaluru Chennai
Hyderabad Jaipur Kathmandu
Kolkata Mumbai

Copyright © Anuj Tiwari 2019

This is a work of fiction. Names, characters, places and incidents are either
the product of the author's imagination or are used fictitiously and any
resemblance to any actual person, living or dead,
events or locales is entirely coincidental.

All rights reserved.
No part of this publication may be reproduced, transmitted,
or stored in a retrieval system, in any form or by any means,
electronic, mechanical, photocopying, recording or otherwise,
without the prior permission of the publisher.

ISBN: 978-93-5333-435-2

Second impression 2019

10 9 8 7 6 5 4 3 2

The moral right of the author has been asserted.

Printed in India by Nutech Print Services

This book is sold subject to the condition that it shall not,
by way of trade or otherwise, be lent, resold, hired out, or otherwise
circulated, without the publisher's prior consent, in any form of binding or
cover other than that in which it is published.

Dedicated to a sister

Prologue

Someone once said that life is all about perspective. But is it really? The first time he punched her in the stomach in the middle of an argument, waves of excruciating pain coursed through her fragile body as she fell on the floor, struggling to open her eyes. In a trivial argument, he left her with severe bruises and an emotional trauma. One punch, and her dreams shattered before her eyes like a house of cards. Such was her dilemma. Her 'prince charming' was not a prince anymore, and was certainly not charming. She tried her best to fix things, but her tolerance had a limit. You can keep shit under your pillow and call it adjustment, but it will stink. Stink miserably. Stink beyond repair. She was not afraid of her broken self. She was afraid of her broken heart. How could someone change so much almost overnight? Her future seemed bleak and she perpetually lived in fear. The same man who had promised to treat her as his queen had turned her into a damsel in distress. His lethal actions knew no bounds. He could do anything—and that scared her to death.

Recalling the past, she tries to think of the good memories rather than the bad ones. If only she had any good ones.

The memories associated to negative emotions overpower her every time she looks at the wire, broom and knife in the balcony. How these sinless weapons have reluctantly tasted every part of her soulless body.

The Sunday morning is foggy, and she is lying on her bed. It is 5 a.m., and she cannot sleep. She is curled up under her sheet. The memories of her sufferings hit her back and forth. They would ask her questions and if she failed to answer, they would whip the soul out of her. She cannot find the energy to confront the challenges of life. Though she is awake, she does not want to get out of bed. She is physically exhausted. Mentally drained. She wonders what is wrong with her life.

She contemplates if she is living or just existing. 'It's tough for me, I can't live like this. If I want to live, I need to make a decision. Otherwise, it's not worth living.'

By now, the sunlight is streaming through the gaps in the blinds. Now awake, she looks tired and her hair is messy. She walks to the mirror, and lightly touches her broken jaws and bruised cheeks. She feels damaged. She thinks of her present, the frustrations that seemed to have gripped her mind. She is unable to think rationally. Her head is throbbing. She approaches the balcony once again, and thinks of her weak defences—this time, unhesitatingly to seek vengeance.

One

The flight, Emirates 503 Boeing 777, lands in Dubai. The brisk warm air of the lively city welcomes Arjun and Dimpy Aunty with open arms. The evening is perky and brimming with possibilities. Arjun is looking forward to meeting new faces and encountering unique experiences in this promising city. He seems a little anxious, but Dimpy Aunty provides the much-needed boost to his confidence. She has been like a sponge that has absorbed negativity and emitted only positivity from the very first day Arjun met her through Anushka—his best friend from college.

Anushka was a year older to him and he remembers the first time he had met her. She was gorging on a hot dog in the college cafeteria. He was looking for someone who could help him with his assignments, and here was this pretty woman. He could not help but stare at her. To his dismay, she noticed it. She felt embarrassed, but could not help smiling back. He liked her innocence. She liked his smile. Something clicked—a bond that was inevitable. That was the foundation of their budding friendship, which bloomed over the years. Although, she still makes him pay for staring at her by treating him like her driver in the beautiful city of Mumbai—a fair price for a friend like her. It may not be visible in their words or expressions that their emotions are intertwined, but, they surely have each other's back.

Dimpy Aunty, a fifty-five-year-old woman and a mother of two daughters, Anushka and Angira, is a vibrant personality, interested in everybody's affairs. Her outgoing nature is in contrast with her husband's demeanour, which is reserved and indifferent to most things apart from his next drink. Despite this difference, there is a warm understanding between them. They are crazy about each other but undemonstrative in their companionship. They are tolerant, easy-going, and battle their way through life with dry humour and a sunny attitude. She believes that a good relationship never gets old, only people do. It is like wine—the older it gets, the better it tastes. They are, what is called, each other's prized possession.

Arjun, on the other hand, lives alone, far away from his family. It is human nature to succumb to love and attention. Moreover, when you are away from your city, you crave friendship, and in Mumbai, Anushka and Dimpy Aunty helped Arjun when he was fighting depression and anxiety for six months. Arjun had not discussed this with anybody until he was found fallen on the floor and people dialled a recent number on his call log, which was Dimpy Aunty's. Since that day, Anushka and Dimpy Aunty help him in his personal and professional life whether he appreciates it or not. The sight of dear ones, their little talks, and their company has the ability to lift one's spirit.

Though Dimpy Aunty acknowledges him as her son, there is a problem. It is evident that he likes Anushka. Isn't it human nature to be naturally attracted to the person who showers you with immense love and attention? Although he has never confessed being smitten with her, over time, their bond has become stronger and now Arjun can count on Dimpy Aunty and Anushka in his life. Though he may not have a long list of people on speed dial, Dimpy Aunty remains the person he can fall back on at any given point of time. That is her relevance in his life—unconditional.

♥

'Do you remember what you said when you went to Kolkata for your first book launch?' Dimpy Aunty asks Arjun. Reminding him of his own words, she adds, 'You said, "I don't think I am that established an author to even get a chance to interact with my readers on a larger platform."'

Arjun laughs, 'Yes, I do. You don't forget things easily, do you?'

'No, I don't. Well, here you go,' Dimpy shows him the way to the entrance of the massive auditorium where Arjun is going to address the crowd that has almost settled by now.

He knows that this experience will enrich him but crowds have always made him anxious. Arjun smiles as if he is the man of the day, which, in fact, he is. Arjun has been nominated for the International Youngest Author Award, Dubai, 2018.

'I still don't believe it,' Arjun murmurs, looking at the crowd, with excitement bubbling within him. The energy is contagious. He can practically feel and hear the high-voltage zinging through the people. Initially, he dreaded crowds but now he feels the enthusiasm and understands the reason behind Dimpy Aunty's constant insistence on attending such vibrant events. A bigger crowd means more book sales, and then she can take all the credit for it.

'Even I do not,' she giggles, 'but it is happening, so live the moment.' Dimpy Aunty looks more excited than Arjun as he gazes around anxiously. It is an emotional moment for Arjun as he has come a long way from where he started his journey. Before he can dive into his past, Dimpy Aunty asks him, 'So, you didn't tell your mother that you have come to Dubai?'

'She knows.'

'And she allowed you to come?' she asks with a glint of amusement in her eyes. Arjun's mother had a long argument with him regarding travelling abroad, simply because she is a mother. Insecurity might as well be every Indian mother's middle name. It had taken him a lot of time to convince her that everything we hear is an opinion, not a fact; everything we see is a perspective, not the truth. So, half-heartedly, she had said yes.

And now, here he is in Dubai.

♥

The human brain starts functioning the moment you are born and never stops—until you stand up to speak in public. Needing the toilet when you don't usually 'have to go' is a typical reaction to pre-speech jitters. 'Why take a chance?' thinks a nervous Arjun. He stands up and contemplates using the restroom before going on the stage.

'Be cool and just chill, and just give your heart a break,' Dimpy Aunty says and he immediately feels comfortable, 'A-R-J-U-N…' she repeats and holds his hand, almost squeezing it.

'Being nervous is obvious but do not pretend that you're too open to sharing all your secrets. Do not be too emotional.

Be decent but don't flatter,' Dimpy Aunty says.

'No doubt my mom feels insecure of me being in your shadow. You are good at convincing people,' says Arjun.

'What I feel is right, not magic. And do not worry, I am not going to ask you to choose between your mother and me,' she winks.

'It would be impossible for me to put you both in the same place. I will just come from the restroom,' Arjun grins at her. He is about to leave for the restroom before his name is announced to come to the podium to address the audience. Arjun is lucky to have two mothers in his life. However, both are suspicious and sarcastic about his actions.

'Do not worry, I'll take the decision on behalf of you whenever your mother needs your opinion,' she laughs and shows him a thumbs up. Arjun proceeds to the restroom in a hurry.

♥

'Please welcome Mr Tiwari on the stage,' the gorgeous woman calls Arjun for the second time and looks at Dimpy Aunty. Dimpy Aunty points at Arjun. Handsome in a white shirt and a pair of denims, Arjun enters the stage. He greets everyone and is welcomed with a massive round of applause. A few beads of sweat are dripping down his neck and back. He has a well-built body, with an athletic physique—broad shoulders and wide chest. He does not just look handsome and fresh, but seems confident, thanks to that radiant smile—that smile which seems to have hidden a thousand tears.

He begins, 'Hello beautiful people, I was just getting

nervous, so I had to convince myself that you are adorable.'

Everyone laughs.

'Before we begin, let me introduce you to the man right in front of you. I am Arjun Tiwari, an author, a public speaker, and an influencer, and it feels great to be called all of these things. However, six years ago, I had a different story, and I am going to share that story with you all today. Well, before I go ahead, I'll start with my schooldays. When I was a kid, I used to tell my mom that I wished to do something different in my life, but every time my mom scolded and slapped me, I would go back to my studies.'

There are some giggles in the crowd.

'Despite that, I still aspired to do something different. What to do was the big question, I was clueless. I grew up and completed my schooling. I will not say my family could not afford it, but yes, there were certain financial issues, so I had to switch my schools often. Until the fifth grade, I studied in a convent school, and then, I was moved to a Hindi-Sanskrit-medium school.

'Isn't it really annoying when you are very hungry, and you have to chant a two-minute-long bhojan mantra before diving straight into your food? We used to do that. If this was not maddening enough, we had pradhanmantri and senapati instead of class monitors and representatives. What were we doing, living during the Upanishads? Well, this was just the beginning, there were many such Vedic style rites we were compelled to observe that were even more dramatic; otherwise, all hell would break loose. Much later, I was moved to a school where teachers were like celebrities; they would rarely come to class.'

Hearing the crowd burst into laughter, Arjun continues,

'Well, those were my early days, sometimes funny and sometimes awful. For instance, once my neighbours forbade their children to play with me and chose to shun me because they believed my English was not proficient enough to match their skills in the language. And then, as years passed, it was time for me to shape my future, a future that seemed bleak. So, what happens in Indian families is that if your neighbour is an engineer or a doctor, you have to succumb to the colossal pressure of being one too. And unfortunately, I had both.'

The crowd burst into laughter once again.

'So, this is where my suspicious mother comes into the picture. Just to let you know, she still keeps track of my social media activities. Considering the return on investment, my mom decided that I should pursue engineering although I was interested in Biology. Well, I left home and started going for IIT-JEE preparatory classes. And for the next ten months, all I learnt was how to be away from family.

'I couldn't clear the IIT, but I got into one of the decent engineering colleges and began my course. Now came the turning point in my life. It was a phase of life that we have all experienced, good or bad. We have all tasted the feeling of being in love. I did too.

'By the way, when you are in love, things look so different, so beautiful—at least, initially. But every coin has two sides, and I never wanted to face the other one. So I started securing my future by writing great things about our relationship and kept it for the doomsday if it ever came, not because I didn't have faith in our relationship, but only because I wanted to be insured. That is why there are companies worth billions of dollars across the globe to give us policies. Because we all want a secured future. Well, things did not work out the way I planned, and I moved to Mumbai with long-time medication for depression and anxiety, and Vitamin D supplements, the cost of which was almost equivalent to the GDP of our country. Eventually, it got so bad that I wanted to end my life.

'It is true that the most complicated thing about broken hearts is that they never look broken. I went into depression and anxiety, a pervasive fear that leads to clingy behaviour, along with a high prescription that the doctor gave me for nine months. Going by the terminology, depression in itself means the intense feeling of severe grief. Yes, I felt dejected. Every part of my body screamed in pain, but nobody seemed to hear a thing. I had become sceptical about things, and I had gotten several check-ups with no diagnosis of my problems. Anxiety sticks to your body like a parasite, and I began harbouring a negative perception about myself and the things around me. That is how you change when you go through a heartbreak. I was a mess, I was broken, I was living a nightmare. The eerie thing about the mind is that you can be thinking of the most intense things but no one else can see them. The world shrugs. Your pupils might dilate. You may sound obscure. Your skin might glisten with sweat. And there is no way anyone can see what you are feeling. No way can they appreciate the strange hell you are living in, or why death seems such a phenomenally good idea.

'Well, those nine months taught me that love does not always guarantee a happily ever after; it sometimes bestows a person with misery and instils a sense of fear just to teach you the right lessons and ensure a stronger comeback. It is like a game of bluff; if you find the right person, it works. If it does not work, move on. Just like in a game of chess, you are not a loser until it is checkmate. However, the question remains, "How willing are you to move on?"

'Moving on simply means freeing yourself from further damage and releasing yourself from unconditional agony, pain and misery. You free yourself from being treated as if you are good for nothing. It is a state of mind where you choose happiness above all. It means that you are prioritizing yourself. It might take time, but you will get there and you will learn to love yourself more.

'Before I could understand this, I, too, suffered a mental trauma post the tragic heartbreak and recurring family issues. I wanted some peace; I tried to heal, I craved to be happy. But I failed. In my heart, I wanted revenge from my neighbours and people who humiliated me in my childhood days, the girl who left me without a reason, and friends who made fun of me because I was an introvert.'

A hush descends over the crowd. The auditorium is filled with silence.

'All this clouded my mind and I desperately wanted to vent, which happened in the form of writing, and I began writing a book with no knowledge of publishing or writing. Many people think if you have written a book the journey is over, but in fact, it has just started. You have to then get it published. So, I compiled everything and started submitting my manuscripts to Indian publishers and they all rejected it because they believed that I didn't know how to write a book. So, what happens in Indian publishing is that if they reject once, there is no chance that the same manuscript will be accepted again.

'Most of you know me as Arjun, also the protagonist in my books, however, my full name is Arjun Kumar Tiwari. And I had sent my first proposal with the name Arjun Tiwari to every publisher I could find. After constant rejection, I worked on my manuscript again for more than a year, and submitted it as Arjun Kumar, hoping they would consider it if I was some other author.'

People laugh. He continues.

'So, I changed my name and tried. Six to seven publishers saw through me, and replied saying, 'Don't try to trick us'. I was happy, at least they had replied. Eventually, after signing a contract, my book was published in September 2012.

'When you are writing a book, it is an emotion, but when it comes out to the world, it is a product. I had to sell my books to share my story, because I knew free stories are never noticed. In Mumbai, we have huge bookstores near Victoria Terminus, where they only keep second-hand and pirated books. So, I started travelling from one part of the city to the other, carrying 100–120 books in my bag. While the shopkeepers earned a margin of 40 per cent on other books, I sold my books at a straight 80 per cent discount. My idea was to venture with a cutthroat pricing policy, and this was suggested by my dearest Dimpy Aunty.'

Arjun looks at Dimpy Aunty and she smiles. Even though everyone is curious to know more about her, Arjun carries on.

'Here, pseudo marketing comes into the picture. If I am getting a profit of X rupees by selling one book, and on the other end, I am getting the same profit by selling two books, as a proactive seller, I'd rather sell just one book instead of two and ensure the same amount of profit. It also takes half the space in the shelf to earn the same profit.

That is how most businesses work in India. Gradually, the news spread among the bookstores, and I started getting calls from neighbouring bookstores. I sold more than 5,000 copies in a month through single-handed efforts, not just in Mumbai but in other metro cities, which is almost the total sales number for many Indian authors. Later, the book hit the bestseller chart, and I was featured among the top five Indian authors, and then you all started noticing.' Arjun smiles.

'So, you must be wondering the point of this fifteen-minute-long speech. Life or people will always give you hiccups and hurdles to stop you, but you need to be determined. It is okay to fall, be a mess, ruin things. What really matters is how strong your comeback is. I always believe that the harder I fall, the higher I will bounce back. In my childhood, my mother always told me two things—life is on an incline, you either go up or you go down, but you never settle, and the second thing she said was that life is so stubborn it teaches you everything that you don't wish to learn.

'So be a diligent learner, and the rest will follow. I think I am in a space where I feel profound happiness in doing anything that I am curious about, irrespective of whether I possess the slightest knowledge about it or not. All I can do is learn and achieve. So just give your heart a break and do not let your curiosity die.'

Arjun exits the stage the way he had entered—with a massive round of applause, and this time there were a few teary eyes. He notices Dimpy Aunty sitting in the front row, smiling at him. He mentally pats his back for the excellent work—that is how he avoids his nervousness. She always gives Arjun feedback after his speech but today refuses to say a single word even after knowing what Arjun has been through. She nods and remains silent. But silences speak volumes. And this time, silence is louder than words. There are still many things Dimpy Aunty wants him to say. That is one of the reasons why she later asks him about his cousin—Addya.

Two

After a wonderful time at the event, Arjun decides to spend some time with Dimpy Aunty, wandering around the bustling streets of the beautiful city. Anushka has given them a long shopping list, and they have to overcome it before they board the evening flight to Mumbai, otherwise disaster is imminent.

It is not unusual for Arjun to spend so much time with Dimpy Aunty. In Mumbai, she always calls him over to her place on the weekends, and this is now a custom for them. Apart from spending the weekend with Dimpy Aunty, he has also become her helping hand in the kitchen. They joke about the fact that even though his mother has given him birth, his humour comes from the lunch- and dinner-table conversations with Dimpy Aunty. Their mutual interest in cooking keeps them connected. For someone else, cooking might be a duty to feed the family, but for him, it is a hobby—a way to release his fatigue. It helps Arjun relieve his mental stress after writing so many drafts of his books.

'Are you not afraid of turbulence anymore?' Dimpy Aunty points out in the evening, as they board the flight. During his last trip, he almost wanted to skip his flight as it was raining heavily in Mumbai. This reminiscence sours his mood.

'I do, but now I have company,' he responds calmly. Amidst the thrum of the engines during takeoff and the vibration caused by the ignition of the aircraft, Arjun tries to distract his mind from irrelevant thoughts. He was, probably, wrong a moment ago. Company does not matter when it comes to fear. The acrophobia remains. He fastens his seat belt and grabs the armrests tightly just as the flight accelerates for takeoff. He closes his eyes, praying silently for a safe journey. The flight gets stable in a few moments, and he looks out of the window thinking about his cousin, Addya.

'What are you thinking about? Anything you wish to share?' With her eyes slightly squinted, Dimpy Aunty questions. Silence speaks when words fail. Taking the hint, Dimpy Aunty decides to remain silent and does not ask further. She knows he will discuss it when he wishes to. No amount of questioning will work on him.

'Nothing,' he winks at her.

'Arjun, I have something to discuss with you…' begins Dimpy Aunty.

This grabs his attention. He turns to her and immediately says, 'Yes, what do you want to discuss? You do not need permission for that.'

'Why don't you tell the truth?'

'Truth? As in?' he looks sceptical.

'Why don't you tell your story? I know your journey has been painful but it is inspiring as well. The world should know it,' Dimpy Aunty gently probes. At first, Arjun ignores her question. She knows that he is shaken by the ordeals in his life but she wants Arjun to tell the truth, apart from the things he was forcefully told to accept. Instead of answering her question, Arjun laughs, 'The story of my life will only discourage people.'

'Hey I am not joking, I am serious. I may sound stupid but I want you to tell them, now that you have moved on and you see things from a very different perspective,' she continues. 'You know, Arjun, sometimes, when we are in love, we become desperate. We do everything possible to keep that person in our life, without giving it a second thought. But everything has two sides.'

Arjun knows that Dimpy Aunty is persistent. The only way to avoid extending the conversation is to accept her assumptions. Arjun knows where the conversation is heading, and so, he says, 'Okay, give me some time to think.'

They enjoy the free drinks on the flight and drift in a deep sleep before they land in Mumbai.

At the airport, someone recognizes Arjun at a confectionary-cum-bookstore where Dimpy Aunty is picking up candies from the shelf. The reader greets Arjun merrily and then he continues looking for his books on the bookshelf assigned to Indian authors.

'Why do they have so many copies of my books? Is that a bad sign? Does that mean no one's buying them?' he wonders out loud.

'Why are you always so negative about yourself? It does not make you sound any cooler, if that is what you are trying to be,' Dimpy Aunty reprimands him.

He blushes, 'I was just curious.'

'Well, then it is surely not the right way to look at things,' she says, and frowns at the same time. 'Despite the fact that your book has been out for a year, they have a lot of copies. That is a good sign. This means they prefer to stock your books due to the high demand. Also, they seem to be selling them at full price.'

'Are you not being over-optimistic? I am sure if I had asked why my books are not available in this store, you would have said that the reason is because they are sold out. Am I not right?'

She laughs. 'No, but I am serious. It's a good feeling, right?'

'Yeah, it's really easy for me to lose perspective on how great my life is. Luckily, I have someone who is always there to remind me. It is still a surreal feeling for me to see my book in bookstores. I do not really process it as something I have written. It still seems like a dream when you see something you have created coming to life.'

'Then why don't you write about Addya?' asks Dimpy Aunty. She knows how to come to the point without letting Arjun know.

'Not sure about her but you are definitely a great character for my books,' Arjun dodges the question.

'That is a bonus for you but I am more serious about Addya. You should write.'

Addya is his cousin who lives in Delhi—someone very dear to Arjun. Though she is four years older to him, she tolerates his incessant monologues at times when he is frustrated and needs to discuss something. Arjun had earlier thought of writing about her, hoping it would help her, but he is wary about talking about her personal life in a society that may never look at her story from her perspective. So, he ignores the question posed by Dimpy Aunty with a polite nod as they exit the airport and call a cab.

The pen is mightier than the sword and it will always be. Arjun remembers what Dimpy Aunty had said yesterday. In a muffled voice, tilting his head slightly away from the pillow, he switches the alarm off and asks, 'Alexa, what's the time?'

'It is 6:55 a.m.,' the robotic voice rings in his ears. Dimpy Aunty gifted him this device on his last birthday so that he could be more punctual and follow his schedules diligently. However, to her disappointment, he has only become more dependent and lazier, carrying Alexa wherever he goes.

'What's my day looking like?' Arjun asks, getting cozier in the sheet.

'You have six reminders.

'Credit card bill.

'Groceries.

'Laundry.

'To drive Dimpy Aunty to the mall.'

'Alexa, stop. Shut up, it's a Saturday and I am on vacation. Alexa, dismiss all alarms,' he shouts, burying himself deeper in his blanket.

'Dismissing all alarms,' Alexa responds.

Lying in his bed, thinking about the moments he has lived after so many ups and downs brings a smile on his face. Reluctantly, he pulls himself off the bed. He frantically looks for something in his vintage suitcase and lays everything on the bed.

Then, he calls Dimpy Aunty.

♥

Morning calls make her nervous and she quickly prays before she picks up Arjun's call. 'Hello Arjun, what happened?'

'Nothing, good morning,' Arjun says from the other end of the line.

'You are calling me at 7:30 in the morning to say good morning; is everything fine?' she reconfirms. She assumes that perhaps Arjun has just called and feels like talking. Even if that is the case, she can sense that something is wrong. Dimpy Aunty knows that Arjun used to talk for hours when he was going through a bad phase but she also knows that is no longer the case; he does not need that anymore. Before she presumes anything else, Arjun says, 'It has been a while since we talked.'

'We met yesterday,' Dimpy Aunty answers in an impassive tone.

'I am taking a day off from work and I want to come over for breakfast,' Arjun self-invites himself for breakfast.

'That's rare,' she says and then adds, 'Only if you make something and don't ruin my kitchen.' She is playful with her words. Ignoring her quip, Arjun comes straight to the point.

'Well, I was thinking about what you said and now it is bothering me. I was thinking about meeting Addya,' Arjun is still not certain about this because when he had discussed writing about Addya with his mother, he had been discouraged.

'Can you come with me?' Arjun asks reluctantly, thinking if he could ask his mother again and convince her that there is no harm in talking about things that have already happened. In fact, it would inadvertently help others.

'Delhi?' Dimpy Aunty breaks her silence. 'Is it about your book on Addya?' she suspects.

'I am still thinking...but I am not sure,' says Arjun.

'That's great news!' she responds gleefully, realizing that she is the first person to know about it.

'I am not sure how either of our parents will react to this. Sometimes, I think, I should not probe things further,' he says.

'Your mother will stop you even for things you are supposed to do because she is a mother and she is protective of you. Rather, overprotective,' she stresses, 'so the best thing to do is to just ask Addya and see if you can convince her. I am sure she'll not refuse.'

'Yeah,' Arjun nods in agreement.

If Dimpy Aunty had been in politics, she would have definitely bagged the role of the external affairs minister.

He continues, 'Also, you wanted me to see your place in Delhi after I shifted here. We have a week. We can roam around, Anushka can also join us. I'll also get a few days off from my work, a much-needed break.' Arjun is smart and a little selfish with her.

'Anushka has to take care of a few things, let her be here. I can only come with you if you can hold my shopping bags.' Dimpy Aunty responds.

'That's what I have been doing so far...'

'Actually, I am not feeling well, you see. Not sure if I can make it...' Dimpy Aunty teases.

Before she can say anything further, Arjun seizes the deal by saying, 'I was just kidding.'

'Well, if we are going, we will leave this Friday. I'll ask him to get the tickets done,' she says; the 'him' is her husband who is the most generous person in the family. Otherwise, one cannot imagine tolerating the ever high-spirited Dimpy Aunty for more than a couple of decades.

On Friday, Air India AI505 takes off for Delhi, giving flight to the lofty ideas of two masterminds who are flying to accomplish the impossible.

Three

Arjun looks out of the cab window. Delhi is always mad and chaotic, and from its roads to the forts to the famous eateries, everything about this city has a unique flavour. They have planned their little itinerary scrupulously. They are very excited to explore the lively Connaught Place. Arjun looks at the beautifully structured houses and the biggest marketplace in Delhi and recalls the experiences he has had here.

'You must have so many memories here,' Dimpy Aunty says, voicing his thoughts.

'Many,' Arjun nods. He looks at her but his thoughts remain elsewhere. At least once in life, there comes a person who changes you for the rest of your life, just like a potter who moulds clay in a shape and bakes it in fire.

'Sir, take us from the Janpath side,' Arjun tells the cab driver. Dimpy Aunty remains silent and does not ask anything. Arjun wants to keep his good memories intact.

'Good memories,' he smiles at her.

'Yes, good memories,' she nods without any idea of what he is talking about.

'By the way, are you planning to change the pair of mismatched socks you are wearing?' Dimpy Aunty notices everything.

'Oh is it?' Arjun checks. 'No, it's the same colour.'
'Yes, same colour but with a different logo.'
'Oh fu…, I didn't notice,' he feels embarrassed.

Dimpy Aunty laughs. Moving through the Janpath market, they reach Connought Place while Arjun changes his socks on the way.

♥

'What if she is not there?' questions Dimpy Aunty, referring to Addya, who has no idea about their sudden arrival and it will be a surprise for her. She will definitely be happy to meet them after such a long time.

'Fingers crossed,' responds Arjun. They have decided to meet her at the gallery she has recently started to curate artwork.

'What happened?' Dimpy Aunty asks.

Arjun realizes that he is meeting her after a long time and he has not gotten anything for her. He smiles and checks for chocolates in his pocket.

'I just got goosebumps,' he murmurs. He licks his lips in anticipation. He does this whenever he is feeling conscious. There is a slight stubble on his face. He smiles. Over the years, he has transformed himself and has begun to look attractive. He remembers how Addya always teased him in his schooldays, when he would secretly give chocolates to her.

'So after how many months are you meeting her?' Dimpy Aunty asks him, taking a big sip of water.

'I think after a couple of months. We recently met at a family reception that I was forced to attend but I eventually had a good time.'

'Did you hook up with someone?' Dimpy Aunty asks whimsically.

'Now I know why my mom tells me to stay away from you. That's good imagination, I appreciate it,' Arjun enjoys sarcasm when it comes from her. Stepping out of the car, hoping the hinges do not creak and squeak, Arjun pulls the door open.

'You have always been a thorough spoilsport,' Dimpy Aunty says, while stepping out.

They hear a soothing music as they enter the gallery. Arjun notices Addya sitting alone in the corner with a pottery wheel, trying hard to make something. Both Arjun and Dimpy Aunty cannot decipher what she is trying to craft. Addya gets up, looks at her hands first, and then walks towards them, screaming, 'What?'

'What what...here I am,' Arjun replies joyfully.

'You didn't even tell me that you are coming...' Addya says, wiping her hands with a piece of newspaper, and comes closer. Her voluminous black hair bounce against her back and her palazzos flutter as she walks. The sleeves of her kurta are folded up to avoid her muddy hands. She smiles gracefully and her face glows with happiness.

Addya hugs Arjun. They have needed this for a very long time. Moreover, she deserves a warm hug for what she has gone through. Everyone falls apart in life, everyone has to go through the worst phase, but getting out of that phase when life seems over takes real grit. Her eyes well up with emotions and she drops her head on his shoulder, 'I am so happy that you have come.'

Dimpy Aunty looks gently at them, admiring the bond they share. Addya is quite similar to Arjun. They are hard workers and have always shared a special bond since their childhood. She feels calm after seeing him. Time changes everything, but Arjun and Dimpy Aunty are certain that it has not changed Addya.

'So, these are tears of happiness, aren't they?' Arjun asks, trying to change her mood.

'Yes! Yes! I am sorry,' she says and wipes her nose and face. She continues, 'You have changed a lot in the last few months. You are looking younger than when I saw you last time.'

'I had an event in Dubai last week. Maybe that's…' before Arjun can complete his sentence, Addya wishes him.

'Oh yeah, many congratulations! Keep making us proud,' Addya hugs him once again before she approaches Dimpy Aunty and gives her a warm hug. She is very fond of her as well.

'I am amazed to see you working so hard and achieving so much. He talks about you quite often,' Dimpy Aunty tells her.

'Life has changed a lot, Arjun. I miss those days and I miss you both so much.'

'But I am always there and if I am not there, I'll always have a backup plan ready for you,' Arjun does not want to speak any further because he knows he will not be able to stop his tears. At times, the harder he pretends to be strong, the more emotional he feels.

♥

The gallery is beautiful and innovative, and probably one of the favourites of the young art lovers in the area. Weekends are generally packed. It is not huge, but the calibre of artwork displayed here is unparalleled, both in presentation and quality. Addya has invested many nights to make the place unique, and she keeps it lively by exhibiting new releases every week. The gallery has curated several notable sculptures. Most of these sculptures feature as the focal point in the room and are not surrounded by glass, thereby enabling visitors to look at each artwork closely. The place is done up creatively and is very different from what she had described to Arjun over the phone.

'How is Anushka?' she asks, pushing her curls behind her ears, while Arjun is busy appreciating the gallery.

'She is fine, she wanted to come but her dad is not well, so she decided to stay back. Well, we decided to surprise you. You look beautiful,' says Dimpy Aunty as she sits on the sofa. Others also settle down.

'Thank you! So, how long do you both plan on staying in Delhi?' Addya asks them. She is perhaps making plans for them.

'Probably, a week or so. I have come to check out my place. I usually visit once or twice a quarter,' says Dimpy Aunty. 'While travelling back from Dubai, Arjun and I had a conversation about your well-being and I asked him why he doesn't consider writing about you,' Dimpy Aunty casually puts the point forward.

Arjun had asked Addya the same thing a year ago. Arjun had presumed that writing the truth on a few social media posts would help her fight the complications of her married life but the situation had worsened so much that she had to leave her home after few months of pregnancy. Her brother Agastya had rescued her from that hell and had protected her endlessly ever since. Arjun was always there to support them. He wanted to write about her—the struggle and the impediments she had encountered in her oppressive marriage, but he never asked again because of Agastya's firm admonishment towards penning down her life, for the society was reluctant to accept those willing to fight against odds and stereotypes.

Her words break the silence, which seems like it has stretched for hours, 'So you will not stop trying,' says Addya. She is more casual with her words now than she was a year ago when Arjun has asked her the same thing.

'Definitely not,' replies Arjun, hoping for agreement in her words.

'Writing a book will not change anything in my life anymore,' she smiles knowingly.

'But it may, perhaps, give some encouragement to many like you,' Arjun sighs. He adds, '…Well why don't you tell me everything from the start, even the things I know.'

'I wish I could give you a diary and you could surprise me with a book,' Addya pulls his leg. 'Let me bring tea for everyone and then let's begin, okay?'

'At your service,' Arjun obeys.

Addya gets up and continues, 'Well, I never really chose to become a curator of art. It was always the creative side of my brain that pushed me to venture into the unknown. I wanted to try but never really had the right resources or the permission,' she laughs.

Though Arjun and Dimpy Aunty have been a part of her journey, for a book to be written, there could be nothing better than her own narration of the events in her life.

Serving them tea, she begins to narrate her ordeals and hands Arjun her diary that he has finally convinced her to share with him.

Twelve Months Ago

Four

All families have traditions, and everyone is expected to follow theirs. Addya, unknowingly, had become a miscible part of this tradition and there was no escape. She did not even know when her family started their tradition. However, one thing was sure—this tradition did not make any sense. Or perhaps it was there to keep Addya in control. She knew that love marriage was frowned upon in her family where everyone had their marriages arranged and that too with massive dowry in the name of gifts and blessings.

She had never understood why people spent their lifelong savings on ceremonies and why dowry was given under the purview of gifts. At times, she questioned her sisters in the family and encouraged them to go ahead and find the partner of their choice. But that never worked and people started complaining to her mother that she was turning into a rebel and didn't necessarily care about the family's reputation or stature. Addya tried to explain her viewpoint to her family but it was all in vain. She crumbled in the face of the love her family showered upon her. She was vivacious, wanted to fly, but conceded defeat before her family's love and expectations from her. Then, her family started looking for a suitable groom and just after a few meetings, wanted that they got married as soon as possible.

It is difficult to decipher if you are getting married to a sane or an insane person. But this is the logic followed in many Indian families—on an average, marriages are arranged after knowing each other for only two weeks. It is baffling. We decide to marry a person after just two weeks of knowing them and spend three months to buy the right wedding dress.

Let us try and analyse this. You meet the person that your family has chosen for you. You are optimistic, assuming that this world is full of great people. So you start talking to that person every day—for an hour or two. Not more than two hours if you have friends, family, work and a life to live. It's easy for a person to pretend to be great for that duration every day. So, you give two hours every day to know that person, and it goes on for months. Then, people in the same family start asking you to get married because you have taken enough time. So practically, you have spent less than four hundred hours with the person, which comes to two weeks. Your life is determined on those mere two weeks of pretentious conversations that you have shared with your potential partner. This is like gambling with life. Shouldn't people be more analytical and take more time before making such life-changing decisions? Addya had taken almost a year to decide if she wanted to choose science or commerce; wasn't this life decision more important than that?

Arranged marriages should not decide the reputation of the family. Raising your son or daughter as a sensible, good human being is what should make a family proud. Unfortunately, like our Indian education system, we are still following outdated traditions that are irrelevant in this era. A 'real' man is not one who pays the bill at a restaurant for a woman and treats her well within the ambit of four walls, but one who is not threatened by an independent modern woman inside and outside—one who isn't pretentious.

Many a times, we follow trends only because others are following the same in the family—baseless traditions, impotent rituals and hopeless customs. It may make one proud to follow these traditions, but we must never follow them blindly. Sadly, the few in Addya's family, who had the courage to fight for their love, were ill-treated by their relatives and were shunned. You cannot choose the family you belong to. Even if she had a choice to be born somewhere else, she would have probably rejected it. She was lucky to be born in this loving family, but it was tricky when everything was secondary to the set values and traditions.

Her family had close ties. Addya was supposed to further the family responsibilities and get married. Her family found Bali, a suitable match for her, and they began talking to each other—even became friends. However, Addya was not in a hurry to get married then—she was working in a giant e-commerce organization in Bengaluru. Later, she had to relocate to Delhi for Bali. She chose this so that they both could spend time with each other. She sacrificed her career to be with him.

♥

Bali was from Delhi, and they became good friends over time. Soon, they became the best of friends, without any obligations or hesitations. Addya started meeting him frequently over the weekends. Eventually, her friends started saying that they were in love, and that was visible on her face. After six months, she realized that she had feelings for him and they started spending most of their time together. Physically, mentally and emotionally, Addya was attached to Bali. She proposed to him because she had always wanted to do this. She never wanted an arranged marriage, so she tried to stretch the courtship time longer. She had seen her friends heartbroken over failed relationships before. So, she took the time to go ahead with the decision that the family had already made for her. Bali happily accepted her proposal. This was a very emotional moment for her. Everything was planned well for her engagement, which was followed by a grand wedding ceremony, in which her family invested most of their savings.

The same family who would be up in arms against anyone who even uttered a single word against Addya turned disobliging after the wedding. When she faced problems in her marriage, they asked her to adjust, and convinced her to believe that eventually, things would get better. After a few months of their wedding, Addya started suspecting that Bali was having an affair, but she was not certain. So, she decided to talk to him. However, whenever she tried to ask something about his work and colleagues, Bali would change the conversation and tactfully comfort her by saying that he cared for her. In fact, she got used to confrontations because she would get more attention during these arguments. Those small fights became the only way Addya could get time from his busy schedule. Otherwise, Bali would be so engrossed in his work that he would not even spend time with her on the weekends. However, those small fights eventually became bigger, and then one day, he punched her stomach in a trivial argument, leaving her with sharp bruises and an emotional trauma. One punch and all her dreams were broken. With pain coursing through her body, she fell on the floor and struggled to open her eyes. What scared her was not that she could not open her eyes, but was how he had changed in just a few weeks. Now, he could do anything to harm her. That shattered her.

Even though Bali had not raised his voice against her in their six-month courtship, everything changed after six months of their marriage. He would get into a fit of rage if she would refuse to have sex with him when she was three-months pregnant. He would curse her often and at times tie her to a chair and beat her indefinitely with a broom. Addya was no longer under the illusion that a 'prince charming' existed.

Addya tried her best to fix things because she knew that everyone would ask her to endure—to adjust. She was an ambitious girl and had her own dreams. She was a gold medalist from a renowned college from Delhi University. She wanted to pursue her dreams and spend her life with someone who could support her. But her life changed when it was attached to someone who had a completely different opinion about 'love'—the term she was fooled with.

♥

Addya never wanted to discuss this with her family, knowing that her brother would have messed things up if he knew something happened to her—physically or mentally. But when you are in pain, you choose a person to listen to your inner voice. Addya chose Arjun—he, who already disliked men who demanded dowry. Many Indian marriages are arranged for either dowry or to satiate the sexual desires of men. The concept of marriage is not sacred anymore. It has become a business, with the son being an asset, while the daughter is considered a liability. The balance sheets are prepared at the time of birth itself. A profit for the one who has a son and a loss for the one who has a daughter. Many people will debate against it but when they peer into their lives and introspect, they will find themselves a victim or a perpetrator of the exact same thing.

After a point, Addya only had the virtual support of Arjun because her in-laws started checking her phone and started asking whom she was always talking to. One day, she found three pages of call details and an RTI (Right to Information) letter about her income. When she asked him about it, Bali said that it was his right to know. He was the same person who had once said, 'I love you more than I have ever loved anyone else in my life,' just before getting married.

Even after so much humiliation, Addya wanted to save her marriage. She did not want to hurt her parents. She lived in pretense for a long time. Her in-laws started making her feel like a refugee in her own house. That upset her, but what deeply hurt her was when they started blaming her parents, Arjun, and Agastya unreasonably. She surrendered several times because this was not new to her. She had already heard from her friends how life changed after marriage. Therefore, she thought that after sometime, this would end. But it was not even close to the end. She became depressed and visited a psychiatrist. When she got pregnant, Addya realized that things were going beyond what she could handle. Arjun advised her to visit her parent's house and discuss this with her family.

She felt disgusted in that environment and wanted to escape. She did not feel like getting intimate with Bali anymore. And then, Bali started forcing her. At times, she felt like she was being raped. However, in this society, it is considered a part of marriage and she had to deal with the ordeal. Her first mistake was ignoring his behaviour, ignoring the first time he shouted at her and hurt her. When someone can hurt you in their normalcy, anything is possible in the worst situation. For her, love was important, and she believed that it came from respect for each other. She had lost it all. Without any regret, Addya decides to run away from Bali, from the everyday torment and pain. She wanted to leave the abusive past behind and start afresh. She was ready to fight them all, with Agastya and Arjun by her side. However, she was unaware of the fact that this gruesome departure from Bali would bring agony to her and her family. It was not long before Agastya found her bruised and shaken after being attacked by two unknown people when she was walking down the street to meet her family. Terrified and furious, Agastya just wanted revenge for what had happened to his sister.

Five

*A*GAStya starts his day unwillingly. He cannot think beyond Addya's situation. He is standing at a podium, in the spotlight. He rolls his sleeve and takes a sip of water before starting. As usual, he flashes his best smile to the audience. This makes them more comfortable with him, eliminating the formality between them. Agastya has completed his master's in finance, but now trains people to function efficiently and live a balanced life.

Agastya visits prominent organizations to stimulate positivity amongst their employees and helps to manage their work-life balance. He is not a traditional motivational speaker or a philosopher who just speaks and exits the auditorium leaving behind dissatisfied minds with unanswered questions. Instead, he is the non-conventional kind. He speaks. He listens. He resolves. Agastya had skipped the idea of studying engineering citing financial issues. Addya was always by his side and convinced him that 'engineering' was not the means to achieve the end. Even those who started their journey with professional courses ended up being authors like Arjun. What was meant to be would always find a way.

♥

Agastya unzips his backpack and sets a glass on the table beside him. He fills the glass with water.

'Half-fill, half-empty.'

Agastya pauses to let his audience consider this. 'Well, I spend the most of my time in the sky and my job is not to train you. I am paid to remind you that you can't perform well in your task if the task is all you do all the time.

'So, I'll not ask you whether this glass is half empty or half-full. You must have heard this already in college and even used this to impress others. Now, you are smarter. Even if it's all empty,' Agastya pours the water back into the jar and continues, 'you will say it's full of oxygen, full of life. Isn't it?' he grins at the crowd.

They laugh and nod their heads in agreement.

'I know it,' he adds. 'We listen to so many things happening around us; it is imperative we learn how to apply what we listen to in our lives. Imagine, one fine morning you begin your day at work, and you see your family members enter your workplace. Slowly, you see your whole family in front of you, including your kids. Will you be able to perform your tasks with utmost efficiency? The answer is "no".'

The audience is listening intently.

'When you take work home, the question remains the same. Will you be able to give your best to your family? They need your attention, not your office work. Isn't it?'

There is applause from all corners.

'Well, well, well, we all spend so much time on what is urgent, that we forget to spend enough time on what is important in our lives. Remember, the word "important" came before the word "urgent". You will have ample of urgent things to do, but reconsider what is more important to you.'

He continues making such relevant points to the audience and ensures that by the time the speech ends, he has made a mark in their hearts and minds. Suddenly, the reminder on his phone rings and Agastya leaves to catch his flight. He drops a message to Addya assuring her that he has not forgotten to get the chocolates from the airport. He will see her soon.

♥

It is a usual mundane morning and Agastya is lying in bed. He has had more than just a tiring evening the day before. Though awake, he does not want to get out of bed. He wonders what is wrong with his life, and how he is going to tell everyone that everything is going to be okay when he is not sure about it himself. Most importantly, how is he going to make Addya believe that he will fix everything? In some or the other way, we all suffer in silence, but we never show it to people. Agastya suffers from major anxiety and is often caught in the middle of unwarranted panic attacks, during which he fears becoming harmful or violent to himself or others.

Thinking about some of his memories with Addya, he falls asleep on the sofa in the balcony, and wakes up cold and shivering. Agastya then returns to his room and before resuming sleep, he carefully examines the prescription that the doctor has given to Addya for her pregnancy. He sets a reminder for her doctor's appointment the next day.

♥

These days, Addya is experiencing a rollercoaster of emotions, due to the ever-fluctuating hormones, changes in her body caused by her pregnancy as she enters her final trimester, and the looming shifts in her life. One moment, she is feeling awful and the next, just marvellous. Today, she wants to paint the nursery blue; tomorrow it could be green or yellow. She is on top of the world, then down in the dumps. It is becoming difficult for her mother—who is over-possessive about her—and Agastya to keep her healthy.

'What if my water breaks when no one is there?'

'What if I don't make it to the hospital in time?'

'Is there something wrong with the baby, why I don't feel it?'

'Or is there something wrong with me? What if I can't breastfeed? Or can't change a diaper?

What if I can't afford college?

What if I don't turn out to be just like my mother?'

Addya constantly faces these questions and self-judgements. Agastya may be perfect in his work, but he tries to be more perfect for her. Agastya and her mother take on the responsibility of her husband. They are pretty good at handling Addya who can go from 'I love you' to 'I hate you' in minutes. These days, she cannot even remember where she parks the car. Occasionally, she leaves the house with the door open—not unlocked, wide open. At times, she wants to go out for dinner, but when the times come for the plan to materialize, she wants to eat Chinese food on the couch, in her maternity pants. At times, she is the happiest and at other times, she cries alone in her room, thinking about everything she has gone through. Sometimes, Agastya is incredibly unsure about his abilities, but he has to be strong and fight his demons, for now he has to support not just Addya but also the little angel growing inside her.

♥

The sunlight is pouring in through the gaps in the curtains. The birds are chattering, and the morning has commenced with many activities—yet everything seems gloomy to him. He has not slept properly in days, but he manages to get up and clean his room before his mother knocks. In the last few days, he has started locking his door before going to bed, which makes Addya a little curious. She expects Agastya to be equally transparent as she shares a special bond with him after her father, who is not there anymore. He was a great man who played all his roles as perfectly as he possibly could. However, now he is in a better place, leaving a void that could never be filled. Agastya has inherited many good qualities from his father and is always missing him, especially in the big events of his life.

Somehow, Agastya has maintained a healthy atmosphere for Addya. He tries to find reasons to get through the sadness but fails time and again. He is at his best when Addya is around but in her absence, the monster is unleashed. He goes to the balcony again to get some air. Thoughts flood his mind and he questions himself, 'Does everyone go through tough times in life? Or it is just me?' Agastya begins thinking about the good memories that Addya always tells him to remember whenever he feels low. There are so many memories, ones that make him happy. Yet, the memories that overpower him are the ones associated with negative emotions. He thinks of his present, the frustrations which seem to have gripped his life.

He is tensed, and his head throbs. He tries to be pragmatic about the future trials Addya is going to face, and to get justice for her, which is rare in this country. He wishes he could tell Bali how wrong it is to torture and ruin someone's life for no reason. He has a plan to seek revenge but he also knows that anything done emotionally might backfire.

Six

*N*obody can predict the future, however, we should not let the past dictate it. These are the words of wisdom spoken by Addya to Agastya, though not always observed. Somehow, these powerful words wilt in front of his present. His friends have always been supportive of him, encouraging him to stay strong, but he finds it exhausting. What if he is unable to fix everything? Who will take care of Addya? His racing thoughts come to an abrupt halt by a loud knock on the door. He places a bookmark, closes the book he is reading these days—*Do's and Don'ts during Pregnancy*—and keeps it on the bookshelf.

'What are you doing standing in the balcony?' Addya steps into the room and inhales a fresh soap fragrance.

'Nothing, I am just trying to follow some yoga tips you gave me,' he beams looking at her. 'But why are you not resting? Come, let's do some breathing exercises.' With an arm around her shoulder, Agastya makes her sit on a chair in the balcony. He continues, 'The doctor has asked you to stop Googling, and start doing yoga for thirty minutes every day.'

'Agastya, you were in bed when I went out for a walk fifteen minutes ago,' Addya replies in despair, shaking her head. She wonders with whom Agastya was talking about her over the phone last night. She presumes it was Arjun; otherwise, she does not like others suggesting plans for her future, making her feel helpless. That is what others have done in the family so far.

♥

Addya and Agastya have been like friends since adolescence. The brother and sister embarked on a new journey of friendship when Agastya shared the incidents of his first relationship with Addya. People share, discuss, find comfort in each other's company, but, eventually with time, these relationships fade into oblivion. Addya does not want this to happen between them and hence, decides to talk to Agastya about it, although she understands that whatever he is doing is out of love and affection for her.

'Were you smoking in the balcony?' Addya asks him in a serious tone.

'I have stopped smoking...it's just that...umm,' he hesitates when he realizes that Addya has caught him.

'Smoking will not help resolve our issues, Agastya. You should not smoke. Please take care of your health. I need you more than anything else and moreover, I want you to be strong ande be by my side,' Addya takes the cigarette box, which he had kept behind the flowerpot when she had stepped in, and throws it in the dustbin kept in the balcony.

'You had quit smoking, hadn't you?' Addya is seeing him smoke after many years. She senses that something is wrong. 'Is everything okay?' she asks and then adds, 'By the way, who was on call last night?'

'Nothing, one of my friends,' Agastya says offhandedly.

The word 'nothing' has all the answers—unfortunately, we ignore it in the hustle of correcting other things. Addya knows how to handle him. However, sometimes, she becomes too persistent. Perhaps, she, too, has become overprotective of him. Agastya does not want to discuss his feelings. He only shows his happy side to her so that she worries less.

She repeats making a guess, 'What are you lurking at, Agastya?'

'Nothing,' he says bluntly.

'I want to talk to you before you leave,' Addya says firmly.

Agastya replies, 'Yes, what happened?'

'That is what I am asking, what happened?' Addya probes him. She suspects that he has become aloof.

'I don't know. Nothing is going fine,' says Agastya in anguish. Addya could see the emotions in his eyes, swiftly rolling down his cheeks.

'Hey, nothing is going wrong. Why are you being so emotional?' Addya hugs him. They need relief and harmony. Having each other helps both of them to stay strong.

'It's okay. It is okay. What happened suddenly? You are the only source of strength for Mom and me. If she sees you crying, she will feel powerless,' Agastya tightens his grip on her shoulder. Even if earlier there was any air of discomfort in their relationship, it has faded away with an earnest hug.

'I do not know. We have had our fights but now I feel that our relationship is on solid ground. Someday, if you call me and I do not pick the call, or you are ill, and I am not there to take care of you, or if you cry and I am not there to wipe your tears, do not just conclude that I do not love you,' Agastya says.

'I'll definitely judge you,' Addya states, passing him the

water bottle from the table. He wipes his face and sits on the chair.

'So, Arjun called you last night? What was he saying?' Agastya abruptly questions. He knows how to switch his words without poking her very well.

Hastily, she exclaims, 'No, he did not call last night, he had called a fortnight ago.'

Agastya does not ask further.

'You know, sometimes I hate Arjun.' The tone of her voice tells him how much she is missing Arjun.

'I thought you admired him the most.'

'Well, I do.'

'Is that because he does not talk to you often?'

'Yeah, maybe. I feel bad about how Mom treated him,' Addya still feels guilty about how her mom had shouted at Arjun when he was asking Addya to move on.

'Maybe he was just being practical, why don't you call him?' Agastya suggests.

'No, I'll wait for his call. He always wishes me at 11:59 p.m. and if he does not this time, then he will be responsible,' saying this, Addya walks out of the room. It is Addya's birthday the next day and she wonders what life has in store for her this year.

Arjun's number does not flash on her cellphone while the hands of the clock inch towards twelve.

Until last year, on this day, everyone would gather at her place or else they would have had to listen to her endless taunts until the next birthday. This year, the stars may not be in her favour. That is okay—she thinks, and with a pause, she gets back to her phone. Suddenly, she hears footsteps.

'Agastya, who is there?' Addya asks, getting out of her bed.

'It's me,' he responds and walks into her room. 'Are you still awake? You should sleep and keep your phone aside.' He fluffs her pillows before she settles down in bed.

'Can you sleep here?' Addya asks rhetorically.

'After I finish my work, yes, but don't make the elephant-march sound,' he laughs and that makes her laugh too. 'Well, listen, I have accepted the invitation on your behalf for ladies' night tomorrow,' he says.

'What? You know Mom will never allow. I have already missed three birthday parties in a row.' Mixed emotions appear on her face.

'You should go out and meet people during this time. It will be good for you, and do not be a pet tortoise. I will talk to Mom. Don't worry about the permission.'

'How many times do I have to tell you that the phone is not good for you?' Her mother marches into her room, already complaining.

'And why don't you tell her not to use the phone?' she turns to Agastya.

'Okay, okay, I'll not, I am going to sleep. Okay?' Addya utters and keeps her phone away on the side table. She is already feeling dizzy after taking so many doses of her medicine. Her mother is just being overprotective. Moreover, she is afraid of someone contacting Addya to convince her to patch up with Bali again and to go back to her in-laws, which Agastya will never let happen now. Her mother takes a round of her room, checking for the basic necessities before she wishes her a good night, and settles for the night.

The door closes. Addya waits for a few minutes for a response to the text message she had sent someone, but nothing comes. With a sigh, she scrolls through the messages on her cellphone before she dozes off.

♥

Precaution is always better than cure and who knows it better than Arjun? Listening to the two humble knocks on the door, Agastya guesses that it is Arjun on the other side.

'I told you to call me first before you knock... Come!' Agastya opens the door in the dark.

'Can't you even switch on the fan? I am dripping sweat here!' Arjun whispers.

Agastya takes him to the nearest sofa, makes him sit, and continues, 'I'll get water for you.'

The door closes, and Arjun looks around the house from the hall. The moonlight coming through the sliding window falls on the photos hanging from polka-dotted balloons, creating a chandelier over the table. It is simply picturesque. Addya, who is currently resting in her bedroom, will love this. The thought brings a smile on Arjun's face.

'This is wonderful,' Arjun is enthralled at seeing a series of photographs from her first birthday to the last year's birthday. Sometimes, a little appreciation does wonders.

Agastya smirks and whispers, 'What else can we do? You are a creative person, you must have ideas.'

Though Arjun is creative, he is a novice in such situations. So, he continues to examine the current scene, 'No this is wonderful. Let us keep it simple. Simple is amazing,' he says and takes the cake out of the bag that he has carefully brought all the way here. Arjun has baked the cake for her. Though he is usually very confident about his cooking, it is the first time he has baked a mixed fruitcake. He wanted to do something special for Addya and hopes that she loves it.

The cake looks tempting with a cherry on top. Arjun lights the candles while Agastya walks towards Addya's room and knocks thrice on the door. Three knocks mean that Agastya is at the door. Agastya has set such protocols for his sister to save her from neighbours who bother her too much and give unnecessary advices. If the number of knocks is not three, it means that Addya can pretend to sleep and ignore people. The door opens. A sleepy Addya comes out of her room, wearing her T-shirt and pyjamas, and cozy slippers. She is touched when she looks at the candles and her pictures, and the cake at the centre of the table.

'Gosh!' Addya exclaims in surprise.

♥

Arjun, Agastya and her mother are standing in the centre of the hall, smiling at her.

'So you have finally gotten the time to come, huh?' she sarcastically looks at Arjun and turns around to look at the wall clock.

'Still a minute to go,' Arjun blinks at her.

She walks ahead and hugs him, not caring about her birthday anymore.

'Wish you a very happy birthday,' he wishes and pats her on her shoulder, leaving no chance for anyone to be emotional on this special day. It is human nature—crisis strengthens relationships. Until we are about to lose someone, we do not understand how precious they are in our lives. Addya always wanted to be surprised on her birthday and, here she is—smiling brightly with her closest people in the room.

'Well, this is something I have specially made for you. I have no idea what expecting mothers eat during pregnancy, so I baked a mixed fruitcake for you. This is the only gift you get from me.'

She laughs, 'A mixed fruitcake. How considerate of you, Arjun. Icing would have made me nauseous.'

'Do not laugh, it is good,' Arjun hands her the knife. Waiting for everyone to settle down, Arjun stands in front of the cake wearing a birthday hat.

'There you go…' they say in unison, as they begin singing the birthday song for Addya.

Addya blows hard on the candle and extinguishes it in one go. With joy, she cuts the cake delicately.

'Who gets the first bite?' Arjun deliberates. He is curious to see Addya's expression when she takes the bite. Though he is not the kind of person who looks for rewards, appreciation for his cooking always encourages him. Sometimes, Dimpy Aunty makes him cook an entire meal just by appreciating his skills—she knows all the tricks.

'What are you hiding?' Addya asks Agastya who is standing between the sofa and the table where the cake is placed.

'Nothing important,' he responds and shoves a paper behind a cushion on the sofa. He cuts a small piece of cake and offers it to her. Everyone wishes her once again.

'This is delicious,' she smiles in surprise, 'Arjun-n-n… mm, so good.'

'Always,' he nods in response, while his eyes try to find out what Agastya has hidden behind the cushion.

Seven

*I*t is around 6 a.m., and Arjun is standing in the balcony while others are sleeping. He unfolds the note that Agastya had kept behind the cushion on the sofa.

Now, Arjun reads what is written in the note.

> I do not know what the future holds, but I was, and I will always be there for you, even if nobody supports you, even if anyone loves you or not. I will make sure that the good days are back, and everything is perfect for you and the little angel who is going to be a part of our life very soon. I know that I have been rude to you at times, and I am not very expressive and genuinely lousy at telling you how much you mean to me in my life. I am sorry if I ever hurt you, trust me, I had no intention of doing so. It is just that anger sometimes overpowers me and I feel frustrated. It may seem a little weird that I have written all this, who does that? But I thought it was important.
>
> I wish you always stay true to what you believe in. I hope you never give up on yourself because I will never give up on you. Remember, no matter

what life throws at you; you, are never alone.

Please remember, you are going to be the best mother ever, and we all love you, including Papa, who is watching all of us from heaven.

'Good morning. Someone is cooking stories,' Addya enters the balcony and looks at him amused.

Arjun turns and pretends to laugh, 'Nothing important, just a piece of paper.' He looks at her cozy slippers that do not make any sound.

'Good morning,' he wishes her and shoves the note back in his pocket.

♥

'How are you up already?' says Arjun.

'Yeah, I am forced to do yoga these days... Why are you up?' Addya asks and sits next to him on the marble platform. This place has witnessed many secrets and memories. Addya spends fifteen minutes every day in solitude, sitting in the balcony after she wakes up, and she does not want anyone to talk to her during this time because she needs her own time. But today, she is more than happy sharing her time with Arjun.

'Just accepting life the way it is. So just going on as usual...' says Arjun.

'Yeah, yeah...good for you,' Addya gestures.

'For you too,' ponders Arjun.

'Not really, my life is so weird. I always thought that I was the stronger one in my family and now it feels like "I" and the word "suffer" have an incessant relationship. I recently came to know that I am suffering from Dependent Personality Disorder,' Addya murmurs. 'You remember, I was a gold medalist in long jump…and here I am, feeling crippled and defeated, unable to disentangle myself from the web of problems entangling me. How things change when we grow up!' sighs Addya.

'Addya! We all suffer from Dependent Personality Disorder. DPD is very common these days. It is just a state of mind where we refuse acceptance and refrain from talking about it. You are unable to take decisions on your own and become dependent on someone for the smallest things. You sense that you are changing. It is harmless if you have a strong willpower. However, it starts attacking your brain cells if you allow your own negative thoughts to lord over you. There is no prescription for it, so you just need to give it time, and right now, you should concentrate on your health.'

'Life is all about perspective. Is it not?' She expects him to answer this.

'Yes, it is. Though we are the youngest in the family, we are adults in our own right. Do you understand what I am trying to say?' Arjun looks her in the eye.

'Yeah.'

'So, we must think, decide and work on what we have decided. You know, even when I write the characters in my books, they do not develop with ease and quiet. Only with an experience of trial and suffering is the soul strengthened, ambition inspired, and success achieved. It may sound philosophical, but it is absolutely true that people value us based on their perceptions and experiences in life. Your best friend will give you the best advice, but everyone has a different perspective. No one can tell you how worthy your life is. It is totally dependent on the point of view one has. Ironsmiths and goldsmiths cannot precisely tell the worth of the same thing. So, you have to convince yourself rather than let others convince you. Life is all about perspective, and you must remember all the important incidents of your life. Isn't it?' Arjun ends his words with the same question mark, but also with some unspoken words of truth.

'You are good at hypnotizing,' Addya says with a smile on her face. 'I am just trying to not give so many fucks in life,' Addya tells Arjun everything that she has not told Agastya because he becomes possessive about her.

'Quite smart, let's go,' says Arjun.

Addya steps inside and Arjun follows her to the breakfast table. Suddenly, he notices something. 'Addya listen! What's that?' he asks. 'What happened to your shoulder?' Arjun bends to examine it but before he can reach her, Addya covers her shoulder with a shawl. Is she hurt? The thought scares Arjun. 'What happened?' Arjun knows her very well. She tries to hide things from him, so Agastya does not come to know.

'Nothing. Maybe some rash.' She pretends to examine her arms to look for the bruises.

'How did you get these?' Arjun asked again.

Addya faces a dilemma; she neither wants to hide nor is she confident enough to tell him.

'It does not hurt,' says Addya. She knows that even though it does not hurt her anymore, it will hurt everyone if she reveals the truth. So, it is better to hide. At least, for the time being.

'Did he hurt you?' Arjun asks, alarmed. She tries not to make any eye contact.

'Don't tell Agastya, please. You know him,' Addya almost pleads with him.

'No,' he replies instantly and enquires again.

'Listen! I am perfectly fine. I have brothers like you and Agastya, and Mom. What else do I need in my life? Right?' Addya knows how from her childhood, they hold on to each other when anyone falls. That is the beauty of a family—the indestructibility.

Addya tries to smile but fails. She almost cries, and to hide her tears, she hugs him.

'Listen! Things will be fine,' Arjun consoles her.

He diverts the depressing thoughts, 'See what Agastya wrote for you last night.'

Addya gently releases herself and looks at the note that Arjun takes out from his pocket.

'He wrote this?' surprised, she asks, and begins to read.

'Yeah. But I also mean it,' Arjun makes her smile.

'That's you,' she reads the note, and the words further strengthen a brother-sister relationship.

Addya enters Agastya's room where he is busy packing his bags.

'So, at what time do you leave tomorrow?' Addya asks Agastya. Agastya is resuming work the next day, after spending a splendid time with his family.

'Early morning at 7,' he says as he takes a bite of a chocolate bar and offers it to Addya. She rolls her eyes and asks with a sceptical look, 'And when are you coming back again?'

'I can come back anytime, whenever you or Mom need me to. Do not worry about that. I am just a call away,' says Agastya, assuring her that they are his priority.

'Still, you cannot take leaves every now and then,' Addya understands how difficult things are for him because of her. He manages everything so well. He tries his best to take care of Addya and his mother.

'You don't need to worry about that,' he smiles in an attempt to make things light for her. Agastya pats her shoulder and says, 'You have to go for some check-ups. Don't forget.'

Agastya gets all her files and prescriptions and arranges them in the right order. 'It's good to see the progress,' he says, giving her the files.

She nods and murmurs a 'thank you'. Addya wishes to ask something but she does not know how he will react. So, she chooses to remain silent. She wants to enquire about Tarjani whom she came to know about, after seeing thirteen missed calls on his cellphone. A casual friend never calls so many times. Is it a budding love interest or something else?

Eight

As quoted by the renowned physicist Albert Einstein, 'When you are with a nice girl, an hour seems like a second. When you sit on a red-hot pan for a second, it seems like an hour. That's the concept of relativity.' Departure from his mother and sister is nothing less than sitting on a red-hot pan for Agastya.

Agastya wants to stay, he wants to be with his mother and sister. But change is the only thing that remains unchanged. And this change is beyond his control; he cannot run away from his responsibilities.

Agastya wakes earlier than necessary, and pulls himself out from between the sheets. He checks his cellphone that is flashing some messages on the screen. The name of the sender brings an itsy-bitsy smile to his hardened face. Ignoring the rest, he replies to just one message—'Hi, Good Morning'.

♥

We are all humans and we all have emotions. If we expect something from someone and we get it, we are blissful but when we do not get what we want, we become disheartened and downcast. Agastya diverts his mind and gets excited about meeting Tarjani in Lucknow before landing to his next corporate session in Bengaluru.

She is an old friend whom he met almost dramatically after four years. There are things that have been happening since the last couple of months that he has not revealed to anyone—not even Addya. Love makes a person secretive. However, you cannot erase memories, you can only make more to overpower them. Agastya tries to forget his past, and reminisces his first meeting with Tarjani.

Agastya knows Tarjani since his college days. They were batchmates. Only a close friend of his knew why Agastya always left for class five minutes early. He wanted to get a seat next to her. He was always afraid to talk to her and that is what most boys do in college and regret it for a lifetime. He instead decided to concentrate on his studies and nothing happened between them in college. However, six months ago, Agastya was waiting at the departure gate for his flight to Delhi from Lucknow. He remembers coming across a woman with a petite figure, standing with her back to him. She had long black and wavy hair. He wanted to steal a glance at her, but his chivalry refrained him from doing so. To his delight, she turned around, brushing her elegant curls against his face, just to flash a fully-lipped smile at him. She stared at him in anticipation. He was astonished beyond words. It was Tarjani. Just when he mustered courage to start a conversation and ask her if she remembered him, the officials made an announcement to commence boarding of the flight.

When he got to his seat, he saw that the seat beside him was empty. He wondered how awesome it would be if she ended up next to him. The years of waiting turned into a blessing for him when a family in her row wanted to sit together. So, she asked the flight attendant if she could take the empty seat beside him. They spent the entire flight discussing everything, right from their college days to their destinations, except the fact that he liked her in college. And then, the flight landed at the Delhi airport. A week later, he got a reply from her to the New Year wish he had sent. That is how his new year started. It has been a few months since they started talking on the phone.

♥

'At what time do you have to leave, Agastya?' his mother asks as she walks out of the kitchen, hands smeared with flour. She calls Addya, 'Breakfast is ready!'

'Mom, what happened? What's special?' Agastya asks her, while Arjun and Addya take their seat around the table.

'Making something special for Arjun,' she says with a sad face.

'Are you making this face because I am leaving?' he asks again, following her from the hall to the kitchen.

'When you are here, I do not have to worry about things, and now...,' her voice gets lower.

'There is no other way, and I can come anytime,' Agastya says. He wants to hug her but he just wipes his eyes, takes a water bottle from the refrigerator, and leaves the kitchen. This happens every time. Whenever Agastya is about to leave, his mom gets emotional.

'What are you thinking?' Addya snaps her fingers.

'All mothers are the same,' Arjun utters. He goes through the same emotions at the time of his departure. 'Don't worry, chachi ji, I will also pay frequent visits. You can call me or

Agastya, we can come anytime,' he assures her, looking at Agastya. Arjun has always been close to this family. Among all his relatives, they are warm, helpful and they do not poke their noses in everything.

'Thanks, beta,' she continues, 'now, sit and have breakfast, you have to leave on time.' She starts setting the table. Introspecting, she follows Agastya to put a few things in his bag. 'This is some pickle for you, and some snacks and sweets. Check it again,' she points at him while he is replying to someone on his phone. He keeps the phone away and listens to her.

'Do you want some?' Agastya asks Arjun.

'I have kept some for him already,' she responds instantly. Agastya keeps them safely as they are now going to be a rare treat for him.

♥

As usual, Arjun rearranges his clothes and sets his hair flawlessly. Addya unlocks the gate of the house. Rasping and screeching at the hinges, the door opens. Agastya takes his bag while checking the arrival of the cab and updates of his flight on his cellphone.

'Do not be so addicted to your cellphone. You all are always so glued to it,' his mother admonishes Agastya.

'See! I have stopped using it,' Addya says, promptly putting the phone in her pocket.

Arjun bids his aunt a farewell by touching her feet.

'God bless you, take care and call us,' she pats his head when he bends down.

'You go inside, I'll leave,' Agastya tells Addya, hugging

her tightly, and murmurs, 'Take care. Remember that you have your doctor's appointment. Take care of Mom too.'

'You too. Will miss you.' The tight grip of her fingers gives away her emotions.

'I'll come soon and do not crave for forbidden things, especially sushi and soft cheese,' he says and kisses the top of her head, hugging her once again. The parting hug between a brother and sister is ineffable.

'Have a safe journey,' she says softly.

The cab speeds away.

The time arrives when Agastya and Tarjani are to meet in person. Post their dramatic meeting at the airport, this is the first time they are meeting. They have been talking over text messages and video calls since the last few months. Agastya wants to make the meeting special and sees this as an opportunity to spend more time with her. After trying on different combinations of outfits, Agastya finally decides on his favourite colour—blue. As he stands in a queue to board the metro towards Lucknow Charbagh Station, he looks handsome in the light blue shirt that fits his broad shoulders and lean frame perfectly. Agastya has an average height and a medium build. With sharp features, a head full of soft black hair, a pair of brown eyes, and an arched brow, he looks reflective, watchful and reasonable. His youthful grin reveals the confidence he did not possess in his college days. He has a look of fatigue, which changes when he feels relaxed or happy, which is seldom these days. His amused and friendly smile exudes warmth and is charming to women. With many thoughts in his head, he boards the metro.

♥

After a lot of planning, he has suggested that they meet at some café, which he hopes is near the airport. However, he must consider her preference first. Whatever little he knows from seeing his friends, very few girls prefer to talk while walking, while some want to talk over a cup of coffee, and some with a glass of wine in their hands. Agastya needs to fit all these in the right order. He is a novice and is conscious while planning such things. First meetings are always like this. While he is excited at the prospect of meeting her, a part of him is also on edge. Though he understands that this is not necessarily a date, he also knows they are not just friends anymore.

♥

Agastya has never visited Lucknow before and all he has heard about it is its remarkable street food. If there are other things he knows, it is because they were described by Tarjani over late night conversations about the city where people carry themselves with grace and give immense respect to each other. People value emotions and relationships in this city. No wonder Tarjani has the same elegance and beauty! Suddenly, all his thoughts come to a standstill when Addya pops up in his head and he remembers how things have changed for her. She deserves a better life and he feels it is his responsibility to make sure she gets it.

While he is immersed in these thoughts, the doors of the metro slide open with an announcement that they have reached Charbagh metro station. Before he can move, someone pushes him out. He looks around and hopes that he sees her first. And then, he notices Tarjani standing in the corridor next to a doorway from which emerges a flickering light. She has a curious style and energy around her, and looks fragile with intelligent expressions. A stunning girl in black trousers and black high-heeled pumps, she has a leopard-patterned scarf around her neck and is wearing sunglasses. Her hair is tied in a ponytail, but a few strands have managed to escape the brutal hold of the rubber band and are lingering around her fragile neck and cheeks. She is fair-skinned, and in many ways, a remarkable creature. She appears strong, self-sufficient, and passionate about her likes and dislikes. In her mid-twenties, there is something about Tarjani's personality—maybe it's her face or just her dressing sense—that is very appealing to Agastya. Agastya recognizes her, but pretends that he has not seen her yet and walks to the other side. He wants to gaze at her beauty a little more before approaching her.

♥

Tarjani takes a few slow steps towards him and calls out, 'Hey, Agastya!'

'Hi, how are you?' says Agastya, trying to sound poised in face of the bedlam around them near the escalator.

'I am good. I hope you were not waiting here for too long,' says Tarjani and gives him a side hug. Agastya was not quite prepared for the hug.

'I am good, not more than fifteen minutes,' he says, thinking, 'Do all guys feel the same on their first meetings?' Even though they are not meeting for the first time, their earlier meetings had been in college corridors or classrooms except the last meeting in the aircraft. In college days, she had hardly noticed him as he had a skinny built and an unremarkable personality then. Tarjani hands him a bottle of water and asks, 'You want anything to eat?'

Agastya looks tired. 'Where should we go?' he asks, even though he has a back-up plan in his mind.

'You tell me, where would you like to go?' Tarjani questions him.

'What about your place?' he says abruptly. Tarjani gives him a look, tilting her head a little.

'I mean where you work,' he clarifies

'I understand,' she says and continues, 'I am pretty sure you will find the place quite interesting.'

They walk towards the exit and call for rickshaw. Tarjani is excited to show him Uzaro.

Nine

'Uzaro—The tiny smiles.'

Agastya reads the name of the gallery just above the entrance. It takes a lot of courage to start something on your own. Most surrender because of the absence of right strategies and motivation, while the rest simply give up, unable to execute their dreams. Tarjani inspires Agastya. Though Agastya is unable to interpret his own feelings, he decides to enjoy the moment with Tarjani. She pushes the glass door and welcomes him in. Cold air greets him and a fresh fragrance of orchids fills his nostrils, lending him an instant feeling of positivity.

'Welcome to my work space, my happy space,' the expressions on her face lightens, and she glances up at the ceiling with twinkling eyes. She loves being here. The woman at the front desk greets Agastya before leaving for the day. Tarjani drags his giant trolley bag and places it beside the desk.

'Thank you,' says Agastya.

♥

Agastya quickly realizes that most of these artworks are the ones she had described over the phone. There is much more to know about her. This gallery is a home to some of the most notable artworks that Tarjani has created. After recognizing her own talent, she sold them at premium prices. She does not have a gigantic collection of art but has around 450 handmade unique masterpieces, beautifully placed in symmetrical rows. One particular artwork that catches Agastya's eyes is a giant abstract made of broken pieces of colourful glass, and the gaps between the pieces are filled by colourful clay. The archives show things that are heartbreaking, and are then beautifully joined back with colours. Every single picture delivers some message. Each one tells a story. A brilliant artist, Tarjani has turned her imagination into beautiful and eye-catching abstracts.

'You want tea or coffee?' she asks, dragging a chair towards the sofa where Agastya collapses after his long journey.

'Tea, please,' he smiles. Tarjani is a tea person too. She laughs and rolls her eyes, remembering some of their older comical conversations. 'Yeah, tea,' she adds.

'Would you like to see the place?' she asks.

Agastya says, 'Why not?'

Tarjani directs him to the area where most of the artworks are exhibited while she makes tea for him in the extreme corner of the area.

Tarjani used to create her artwork sitting on her kitchen floor during her college days. Now, that kitchen has turned into her cabin where she spends her day bringing her imagination to life. In fact, this is the only part of the gallery where there is any daylight for her to dry her artwork. This place is the epitome of creativity—in contrast to her emotional turmoil caused by the accident her brother met with, putting the whole family in a trauma. He encouraged her to initiate this unique idea. It is obvious that he cares for her and he gets worried at times when she takes too much pressure on herself. After all, it is difficult to do everything single-handedly.

'Isn't it too much to handle alone?' Agastya asks her.

Tarjani smiles, 'Manageable.'

'Still.'

'Actually, I feel more comfortable doing things on my own. It gives me a sense of pride and independence. Moreover, I am not alone,' Tarjani smiles and points at the reception where Agastya had met the woman. Agastya fiddles with the diary kept on the hand rest as Tarjani places two teacups on the centre table. Agastya passes a cup of tea to her side of the table. She tears the sugar pouch and pours it into her cup. 'You want some sugar, too?'

Mulling over something, Agastya politely refuses.

'Why don't you come to Delhi?' Agastya tells her. Maybe he is insistent so they can spend some more time together. Agastya had asked her previously too but she has always prioritized her work and family in Lucknow.

'You never shared anything about your past,' Agastya asks the same question he has tried to ask many times during their late-night conversations.

'There is nothing to share; it is similar to everyone else's. We all have a past, we were all left alone to cry, and to wipe our own tears when we were done crying. And then, we curse the time that has passed and wait for the pain to heal with time. It will take me a long time to tell you everything,

I am sure you do not want to spend time that way.' She raises her chin and squints at him.

'Okay,' he nods.

'Please do not misunderstand, but, you see what I have done. This is quite productive, isn't it?' she gazes at him.

'That I can see,' he appreciates and then asks, 'how's Aarav?' He continues, 'I did not ask you about your brother over the phone because this is something I wanted to know when I met you in person.'

'Yeah, he is doing fine. We were discussing about your epic session failures, and how you encouraged people to achieve a work-life balance,' Tarjani laughs.

'Yeah…early days of my work,' Agastya murmurs with a sarcastic smile and then he asks again, 'So what happened to Aarav?'

'I was eighteen when he met with an accident while returning from his basketball session. The day the phone rang, and I heard my mom say cryptic words like coroner, needle, autopsy, was the most heart-wrenching day of my life. I could barely breathe. I could barely stand. Desolation engulfed the entire family. In the thick of the trauma, I did not apprehend that the rest of my life would change forever. He was now on a wheelchair. I tried to remain strong, but inside me, something broke. I lived in a daze while people passed me by, offering solace, words and hugs to him. That day, it truly dawned upon him that he was disabled.'

Tarjani continues, 'It was the same year I used to go with my mom for her chemotherapy sessions in Mumbai. She was suffering from cancer.'

'How is she is now?' Agastya asks her.

'Both are better now. Mom is still on medication but

she has almost recovered. My brother's disability was a blow for everyone. My family had such high hopes for him, and in a moment, everything was in shambles. Life was testing us constantly but it was I who took a stand for everything because I had to. My parents gave me the liberty to be a girl without imposing any restrictions on me. They were kind enough to leave everything and allow a fresh start for the four of us. We shifted to a new part of the city—away from all the miseries. It was a drastic change for all of us.'

'Everyone goes through tough times; we just need to have courage. Even if we fall down sometimes, we must bounce back again—to greater heights. Even a hurricane subsides after some time,' he says, placing his warm hand on hers. He then holds her in his arms and they sit silently on the sofa. He can relate to her story after the pain he has been through with his sister.

'I am fine,' she says. The corners of her eyes were wet. Tarjani closes her eyes to holds back her emotions. The silence is almost palpable—no swish of clothing, their breathing slow and barely audible, not even a hush breaks their silence. Her eyes dart towards him.

'Let's go upstairs if you're done with your tea, I'll show you some things,' says Tarjani, getting up and trying to distract herself.

'Sure.'

With each step Agastya takes, he is empowered by her words, and then he thinks of his sister who is suffering. A great job or a great education is not the only thing that makes your career outstanding; it is also about finding the right person at the right time who encourages you for the rest of your life. We must respect each other in a relationship, which is rare these days. It is about empowering each other. Agastya wishes he could have met Tarjani earlier. He would not have to fight alone for Addya. This companionship would have helped them heal each other.

Tarjani is beautiful without knowing it and possesses a charm that she is unaware of. Agastya realizes that her beauty is the least impressive of all her qualities. The deep connection they have shared and the peace and balance it has brought to his life beats physical beauty. While they head upstairs, Agastya thinks about how he is going to convey his feelings to her. He loves her. He also knows that in this modern world of easy relationships, falling in love is the easiest part of a relationship; the real struggle starts when you both have to make efforts to keep the spark alive. He does not want to take any risk and no amount of preparation ever suffices. So, the best way is for it to come naturally. Being raw lends simplicity to love. Agastya decides to be real.

Tarjani switches on the lights and Agastya looks at the room and exclaims, 'This place is amazing!' Agastya is mesmerized to see the artworks hanging on the wall.

'Thank you,' she grins and continues, 'you know what, it was pretty clear from the beginning just how different my brother and I were from one another. He was chatty, I was quiet; he was outgoing, I was an introvert; he was bossy, I was meek. However, he was my childhood's keeper. The person who was supposed to walk with me longer than anyone else in this life. In our childhood, when our cousins would come for a vacation and break our toys while playing, Aarav would glue them back—just like the style of these artworks—and this would make both of us happy. Back then, I used to laugh at his foolishness, but now it is my only companion when he is not around. Never had I thought in my wildest dreams that I'd churn my brother's hobby into my profession. Inspiration can come from anywhere when someone means the world to you.'

'I completely agree,' he looks at her standing in the extreme corner of the room. His fingers move towards the switches and now darkness is their only companion.

'Gosh! What happened?' Agastya says, standing there.

'Let me check,' answers Tarjani as she blindly takes steps with the help of the wall.

'No need,' says Agastya.

'Just stand there,' Agastya simply utters these words. He pauses to think. There is a sense of uncertainty in the air. Tarjani agrees, without saying anything else. She has not moved a step closer to him. Agastya takes the initiative. He walks to her. He breathes in her scent and takes her soft hands in his own.

'I wish I am not too late. I have liked you for more than five years. I admit that I was aware of your every move in college, and you were clueless about it. I don't want to waste any more time.'

'You were weird then, Agastya. You could have at least

initiated a conversation, and you spent years just silently liking me,' articulates Tarjani.

He gingerly touches her quivering lips. He kisses her tenderly. There is no uncertainty between them now. Love takes its own course. She holds him tightly in her arms. Neither of them wants this moment to end. Love is not the spark two people feel when they see each other, love is peace and the feeling of wholeness they both feel when they are holding each other in silence.

'I know you are heartbroken, so am I. But we still have a heart, we still breathe, and it's not cheesy at all to say that I want to breathe the same air with you. Would you like to grow old with me?' says Agastya.

'You have already kissed me, this should have been asked before that. Right? I love you.'

'...and the best is yet to be.' They say together, echoing the famous words of Robert Browning. Tarjani releases him from her embrace and walks back to the switchboard. The light dawns upon the new couple in the room.

'Can't you stay here today?' Tarjani asks Agastya as they go back downstairs and sit on the sofa. She wants to spend more time with him. These moments are rare and she wants to make the best of them. Agastya checks how much more time he can manage to spend with her. He replies to Addya's message, asking about his journey. According to Addya, he must be reaching Bengaluru this moment.

'Well, I have an event in Guwahati towards the end of this month, you could join me if you want as you have always been curious about my work,' she tells him excitedly and invites him.

'That's news.'

'They are sponsoring it with a few perks; we should encash it,' Tarjani looks at him, full of hope.

'What exactly is it?' Agastya enquires in excitement.

'So, I was referred to Vivanta by Taj and they want a piece that can match their interiors. So, I just need to make something specific.' This is not new for her as she has created innumerable pieces before. But this is a big project that can make her stronger financially and she can finally make her dreams of an expansion come true.

'That's cool. I used to feel that I work too hard but it all seems delusional now that I have met you. I'll come with you,' he agrees.

'That's not true,' Tarjani's smile reaches her eyes.

'So, what are you presenting to them?' Agastya is curious and looks around the gallery.

'They just want to discuss and see the album, but I have been asked to create something distinctive. So, let's see what they demand of me,' says Tarjani.

Agastya is pleased to see her delighted. Suddenly, his phone vibrates. Agastya looks alarmed as he looks at his phone hysterically.

'What happened?' Tarjani asks. There is something Agastya has not shared with her. Creases form on his forehead and he starts sweating. Tarjani gets anxious and stands next to him.

'What happened?' she asks.

'We received a legal notice to be present at the court next month,' says Agastya as if everything that happened a moment ago feels nothing.

'But she is pregnant, right?'

'That's why they are troubling her again and again. I am ashamed that such people still exist even after being educated.'

'Tell me if I can be of any aid to you or Addya. Just have patience and faith. That's what I have learnt.'

Agastya is no longer as happy as he was moments ago, but he feels stronger than he has in a long time. He distracts himself from negative thoughts, and saying goodbye after promising to see her soon, he leaves to catch his flight to Bengaluru.

Ten

At the airport, Tarjani is checking out some Russian artwork. There is a stranger checking out the tiny gallery as well. He strikes up a conversation with Tarjani and asks her what she does. She shows him her work and he seems tremendously impressed by it. He immediately gives her a purchase order for a few art pieces. Agastya always wanted this—for her to speak to as many people in the art world as possible and gain contacts. Agastya knows this works because he shares how Arjun used to sell his copies visiting bookstores frequently and enquiring desperately about his books.

Agastya says, 'Arjun had once asked a bookstore so many times that the next time he passed it he saw a pile of his books at the bookstore. He even had a small meet-up with his fans at the same bookstore.' Arjun always tells Agastya that being consistent with small efforts is the key to success.

'He is crazy. I have read one of his books. I would love to read the rest too, they seem inspiring,' says Tarjani.

'See! That's how it works, now you will read his books. I have helped my brother sell at least one copy of his books whenever I have gone out with him by talking randomly about his books. He thought it was embarrassing but now when you meet him, you must ask him. He feels proud. One day you will too,' laughs Agastya.

'I will,' she says with certainty.

There are white clouds in the blazing blue sky. It seems like a pleasant evening. The trees look fiery with autumn colours. There is an air of eagerness and the weather is pleasant in the beautiful city as they step into Vivanta by Taj, Guwahati. It is as if nature has set up the perfect ambiance for Tarjani's meeting. The afternoon is brimming with possibilities. Tarjani is visibly excited in the anticipation of the new process of creation and collaboration, and probably, a big new project to be able to work harder on. This profession has made her a frequent traveller, and she has met many accomplished people because of it. She believes that when problems knock at our door, we get a thousand opportunities to know our hidden strengths. Moreover, it is just about stepping out of the comfort zone that enables us to attain extraordinary things in life.

'May I have your I.D. please,' the generous woman at the front desk asks him.

'He is with me. I have an appointment with Mr Bharali. Can you please check?' Tarjani asks gracefully.

'From Lucknow...' she smiles at Tarjani and Agastya.

'Yes,' Agastya responds. She hands them the room keys. 'Thanks, Charvi,' Agastya says, reading the name from her employee badge.

'You're welcome, have a wonderful stay,' the soft musical voice fades away as they proceed to the lift in the lobby.

Tarjani and Agastya reach the hotel room. Agastya hauls her trolley bag through the antechamber to the room. The foyer leads to a sitting area furnished with a sofa, armchairs and a tea table. With a sponsored flight ticket and stay at a five star, this is a much-needed break for both of them. Pulling the curtain up, Tarjani picks up the check-in slip from the table and enters the password to connect to the hotel WiFi. Walking towards the window, she checks some e-mails while Agastya examines the meticulously decorated room that includes a cozy bed and a sitting area in the balcony. They are going to enjoy the three-day stay tremendously.

After an hour or so, Agastya is lying on his stomach, wearing a bathrobe, while Tarjani steps into the shower after the long journey. He is reviewing his sister's report on his cellphone, which says that a week has been extended for her delivery. He opens the legal notice document that is to be presented to the court next month—the date clashes with her new delivery date. Agastya informs Arjun and waits for him to read the message.

Agastya sees Tarjani come out of the shower with a towel wrapped around her lovely body. She is wearing cute bedroom slippers with pom-poms. On her left ankle, there is a gold anklet. She looks incredible.

'What?' Tarjani probes.

'Nothing,' Agastya smiles at her.

'Then pass my gown,' says Tarjani.

'Sure,' Agastya gets up and passes the wine-coloured nightgown to her. Tarjani tries to read the expressions on his face.

'What?' he asks when he sees her staring at her.

'Thanks for coming with me.' She feels happy in his company.

'Always!' he says.

♥

Looking like a dream in the wine gown and LaPerla lingerie, she approaches him gingerly. He gently kisses the top of her head and pulls her closer to his body. Tarjani slowly looks up to meet his lips in a soft kiss. Agastya takes in her sweet scent. In a tight embrace, they are intertwined together, almost squeezing the breath out of each other.

'I'm exhilarated,' he says, and then reaches over to play with one of the straps of her lingerie. He wishes to go beyond, and grabs her tightly.

'Agastya…'

Agastya slowly runs his finger along her spine and then traces it all the way down to the bottom. He then starts kissing her body, inch by inch. She can feel the feather-light brush of his mouth against her skin in places she cannot see. She just senses the movement on her skin. His hands slide down her body, and she watches his face while he playfully touches her fragile parts—her neck, her back, her soft belly. She cradles his shoulder as he runs his calloused palm all over her—sandpaper meeting velvet skin.

Her carved shoulders drive him insane; he embraces her, and she lets him.

'I love you,' she says, closing her eyes. Agastya has promised her beautiful love. They already know each other's stories; now they subside into silence and sweet anticipatory thoughts. And then, he rests his head against her. With her, he is at ease, and everything feels right in the world. He kisses her again, slowly undressing her, his face hidden in the curtain of her gown. His hands touch every part of her body. His lips gently kiss every part of her. She feels a little alarmed as the garment slides from her body. But his slow rhythmic actions comfort her. Then, she experiences a sharp, brief pain and a sweet spasm coursing through her body. She seems to rise in the air without any more pain, just sweetness, feeling incredible. Breathless, Tarjani presses herself hard against him. Their love is undeniably beautiful.

She whispers into his ears, 'You know, there is another reason why I love you.'

'Why?'

'Because I have never seen a bachelor reading a book titled *Dos and Don'ts During Pregnancy*,' says Tarjani. Agastya feels embarrassed for a moment as he remembers holding the book while waiting for Tarjani at the metro station, and then they both laugh. They are filled with pleasure and crash into each other's arms. It truly is a memorable night for them.

Next morning, Tarjani begins her work for the project. Agastya wraps up his assignments as well and makes some calls. He wants to finish his work so that he can spend time with her once she is done. He pours water in a glass and hands it to Tarjani, 'Have some water.'

'Thanks, I needed this,' replies Tarjani while working on a project.

'Are you busy?' she asks him.

'No.'

'Then why don't you join me?' she calls him.

'I thought I shouldn't disturb you because you said you need your space to work,' he says.

Tarjani laughs. 'Never mind that. I would be happy if you help me.'

Though Agastya does not know what exactly she is making, he decides to help her by following her instructions.

'You can tell me what to do,' says Agastya sitting beside her on the floor.

'Cool, so now I have a helping hand. Can you paint this for me?' Tarjani hands him a cardboard and passes the brush and colour. There is no creativity required here; he simply has to paint the board. Yet, he feels he has to form a good impression.

'Okay,' Agastya nods and waves the brush in such a manner, it seems like Leonardo da Vinci has come back to life in the twenty-first century.

Tarjani looks at him and grins.

'I have been doing this all my life but I still love the smell of fresh paint every time I work,' Tarjani smiles at him.

'Will this light do? Don't artists need good lighting?' he asks.

'This works for me,' Tarjani states. She puts her pencil down and sets her sketchbook and drawing materials on the floor, slowly bringing the abstract to reality on the wooden frame. Trying to forget her nervousness while working on one of the biggest projects of her life, she sticks stones and clay to fill the gaps, for which she is known in the city. What emerges is the best thing she has ever created. Her pose is languid, her hands beautiful, and her eyes radiate energy. She is lost in brushing soft colours and wants to finish it on time so that it can dry. The day after tomorrow is a big day for her.

Tarjani washes away the paint from her hands. 'I need a break,' says Tarjani, scrutinizing her work.

'You want tea?' asks Agastya.

'If you make it,' Tarjani says.

'I have only made tea for Addya and she has never complained. So, if you are okay with it, I can make some. Or else, we can order,' he says.

'I think, it's better to order then,' she laughs.

'Hmm...hmm,' Agastya nods and asks, 'tell me one thing.'

'Yes.'

'You love your work...'

'Without any doubt,' she blinks at him, 'to a point where I can give up anything to pursue my art. I know this is not always the right approach, but when Dad was out of money due to my mother's treatment, this was an additional source of income for us. Some things become very important in our lives because they were incidental to certain important events.'

Agastya whispers in her ears, 'I feel blessed to have you in my life. I have only seen broken things around. Broken relationships. Broken people. I am glad I have you now to glue them back together and give them the best possible shape. I am deeply in love with you. You know what, you are different from me—your work, your thoughts, and your passion. It is true that I still do not know many things about you, but I am in love with the things I know. I will always remain by your side. You just need to stop pulling my leg about the types of books I read these days,' he adds, making her laugh.

She glances at him and wraps him in her arms. She says, 'I love you too, and I just want to love you forever. I wish you stay by my side for eternity because I don't think I've the capacity to face heartbreak.'

Holding her tightly, he turns and softly kisses her on her cheeks. 'Sometimes, things might not go as intended, but they turn out to be even better. In the toughest situations, you just need to give your heart a break.'

Suddenly, Agastya's cellphone rings. It is Addya.

♥

'Hi, Addya,' he says, getting up and walking towards the window. Tarjani's eyes follow him.

'Hello Agastya, this is Addya's friend. Addya is not well, so we have come to the hospital. Can you come? Aunty really needs you here,' she speaks as if she is in a hurry.

With a racing heart, he asks apprehensively, 'What happened to her?'

Tarjani walks up to him once she senses something is wrong. She stares at his face, trying to decipher the situation.

'She's in the hospital…' Addya's friend says on the phone. 'She has been vomitting a lot since morning and we had to bring her to the hospital.'

'Which hospital?' he asks her.

'Indraprastha Apollo Hospital.'

'I am coming. Please take care of Mom and Addya. Call me if anything is needed. I am coming there,' Agastya says in a wobbly voice.

'Your cousin has come, but you also please come...'

'Yes. I am reaching there, just take care of her please,' Agastya almost pleads. He finds himself in a downward spiral of anxiety. He disconnects the call and starts checking for the next flight to Delhi on his phone.

'What happened, Agastya? Is everything fine?' Tarjani squeezes his palm in impatience.

'Addya is not well, I need to go. I am sorry I can't be here with you,' he tosses his belongings into the bag in haste.

'Should I come with you? I can take this up later,' Tarjani does not know what to say but responds with the first thing that comes to her mind.

'No, you take care. I need to leave now,' he scrolls down on his recent call log and taps Arjun's number. Then, he leaves for the airport, opening the door in a fluster.

Tarjani almost runs after him, watching him look for an autorickshaw outside the hotel. The woman at the front desk stares at him and then at Tarjani. She is unable to comprehend the gravity of the situation.

'Ma'am, is everything alright?' she asks.

'Yeah, can you call a cab?' Tarjani asks her anxiously.

'Sure. Just give me a minute,' the woman dials the number and calls for a cab. But by then, it is too late. Tarjani watches Agastya take an autorickshaw and speed away.

Eleven

Shifting restlessly on the bed, she vomits whatever she had eaten last night. Arjun holds her. She clasps his hand tightly and says, 'I'm okay. I just need something to drink. I feel dehydrated.'

'Can she have juice or something...?' her worried mother asks the nurse, who is monitoring Addya's heartbeat on the cardiac monitor. There is an IV drip attached to inject medicines and fluids in her body.

'Do not give her anything, just some water. Not much, only a few sips. The doctor is coming,' the nurse replies, injecting the medicine in the saline bottle. Addya leans on the headboard of the hospital bed. Her mother gives her some water in a glass. She rubs Addya's back to make her comfortable. She takes a few sips and the next moment, she pukes again. Only this time, it is blood.

'Someone call the doctors...' Arjun screams and looks terrified. He is constantly calling Agastya. Arjun runs to call the doctors and her mother takes her in her arms, 'The doctor is coming... The doctor is coming!'

'Mom, my stomach hurts. I can't tolerate the pain anymore!' she shouts, squeezing her mother's hand tightly. With tears flowing, she groans and flinches in pain.

'Nothing will happen,' her mother kisses her forehead.

'The doctor is coming,' Arjun says as he enters the room again. A doctor arrives with two nurses. One puts the oxygen mask on her face and the other examines the growing fluctuations on the cardiac monitor. One more doctor joins them and starts giving different types of drugs through injections to alleviate the pain. The nurses request Arjun and her mother to go out.

'We need to take her to the ICU,' one doctor says to the other.

When Addya wakes up, she notices she is in a strange green room with no windows—only overhead surgical lights. It looks like an operation theatre. Everything is in dull grey and heavy blacks. Addya can feel her pulse beating, blocking out all other sounds except her breathing, which she is raggedly drawing at short intervals. She cannot take her eyes away from the group of doctors and nurses in the room. She wants to speak, but is unable to move her lips. At least she is alive. Nothing else matters. She has always tried to be brave, even in awful situations, but right now, she is scared and feeble. She can feel blood flowing on her thighs. Nurses and doctors keep coming in and going out. Then, a kind woman calls Dr Thomas who is a surgeon and is going to perform an emergency surgery on her. This is what Arjun has been told too. The doctor walks in the room with Dr Shripath, perhaps the assistant doctor, and checks her heartbeat and blood pressure.

Arjun is standing outside the operation theatre, praying for her life. He straightens his face and tries to hide his emotions but in vain. Arjun suddenly sees Agastya climbing the stairs two at a time and running to find the ward.

'Agastya,' screams Arjun. Agastya turns and runs towards the room. His hands are shaking and his face is white as a sheet of paper. He is mentally willing her to stay strong as that is what they have always promised each other, even in turbulent times.

'Why are you standing here? Where is Addya? I want to meet her. How is she now?' Agastya asks a number of questions, one after the other.

'She is in the operation theatre,' Arjun says apprehensively.

'Can I see her for a minute?' Agastya questions.

'They are going to perform a surgery,' Arjun repeats the words of the doctor.

'Surgery for what? She is just eight months pregnant. Why did you consent to it?' an alarmed Agastya asks Arjun and then turns to his mother.

'She is in a critical condition, it has to be done,' his mother responds. Her mother is praying for her well-being.

'What?' Agastya exclaims, as a sudden feeling of emptiness hits his chest and a chill runs down his spine.

'Arjun...please,' Dr Shripath calls Arjun, coming out of the operation theatre. Everyone runs to him.

'She is going through pre-eclampsia and her blood pressure is shooting up, which can damage her brain and other organs,' he tells them as he hands the consent form for the signature.

'What's this?' asks Agastya.

'Just a formality before we proceed with the operation,' the doctor explains. Arjun hands over the paper to Agastya.

Agastya reads a few lines and signs with trembling hands. The doctor takes it and goes back to the operation theatre. Agastya tries to see through the gap of the door that is ajar for a moment. She is lying on the bed and the lights are dim. He receives a gust of sterile chemical sanitizer and then the door closes. He knows that Addya is going to hate him if he ever tells her the truth—he did not even think for a moment before signing the consent form to save her first before the child in an irresolute situation. Maybe he is being selfish but that is his love for her—unconditional.

Agastya is numb and sits on the sofa next to his mother.

'She is going to be fine, do not worry,' his mother consoles him.

Agastya sniffs and puts his head on her lap. She has never seen him so frail. Once the first tear breaks free, the rest follow in an unbroken stream. His mother is devastated to see both her children in immense pain.

'It's okay. Your mother is always here for both of you. Everything will be fine,' she wipes her tears and calms him down.

'Please, can I see her? Please just once,' says Agastya, looking at Arjun.

'You cannot meet her. She is in the operation theatre. When she comes out, you will be the first person to meet her, okay? Just give them some time. She is going to be okay,' Arjun pats his shoulder.

♥

Agastya sits outside the operation theatre until sunlight pours from the blinds in a few hours, trying to hold himself together. He feels pain he has never experienced before. His mother tries to console him by telling him sweet stories of their childhood. She reminds him of the way they took pleasure in small things, even as greater things crumbled. As children, they would seldom give any thought to their future. The innocence then had kindled immeasurable delights, which was seldom the case as they grew into adults. As kids, their happiness knew no bounds. Some relationships are not defined in any book—they can only be felt. Each one of them is feeling that indestructible bond right now.

Suddenly, the door opens and Agastya impatiently approaches the doctors.

Twelve

*I*t is so surreal. He knew that she was in labour but it is now that the reality hits him—when he holds the baby girl for the first time in his arms. He is exhausted but overwhelmed and very much in love. A part of him cannot believe she is actually in his arms. Being the younger one for the past twenty-eight years, he feels older and responsible today. While the trials and tribulations of childbirth are well known, what happens to mothers after they go through the painful and occasionally traumatic process is something only they can comprehend.

Addya hears Agastya's voice faintly. They say that childbirth is an experience that changes a woman's life forever, and for the better. Addya is exhausted, yet a victorious smile is plastered on her face. Her eyes are brimming with tears. She holds his hand meekly. Agastya looks at her pale face and there is a glimpse of ecstasy and gratitude in her eyes. Strong families are able to withstand and rebound from disruptive life challenges. The perfect family is not a myth anymore.

The doctor enters the room and congratulates everyone in the room, and looking at Addya, he says, 'You are one of the strongest women I have treated in my career.' He glances at the little one and says with a meaningful smile, 'She is a miracle child. Have you thought of a name?'

Addya looks at Agastya and her mother and says, 'Takshika.'

♥

It is a joyous occasion. Words are not enough to articulate the rollercoaster of emotions each one of them is experiencing. Addya protected Agastya for years and then came a time when he started protecting her against all odds. He became her backbone. They share such a strong bond that it makes him want to shower her with love. He knows that he can do anything to protect her. Agastya bends down and hugs her, almost squeezing the new family member in between. He says, 'It's time to get back to work, together.'

Addya hugs him back tightly and says, 'Thank you!' He pats her shoulder and they remain silent for a moment. And then, he says, 'Childbirth is an experience that changes a woman's life forever, for the better.'

'…and it is going to change your life too. Be prepared to clean nappies,' she tries to laugh. 'By the way, did you read that in the book?'

'Yes, the first book I have finished in my whole life apart from the ones related to corporate stuff,' he chuckles.

When Arjun and her mother are out consulting doctors, Addya asks him, 'Why didn't you tell me about Tarjani? How's she?'

♥

Though Agastya had told Addya that he had a crush on Tarjani in one of their conversations about college days, he had not told her about their reunion. When she had seen the number of missed calls in his cellphone, she had guessed that something was going on between the two.

'She is good. I was not sure if things would work out between us. So, I wanted to be certain before I could tell you about her,' Agastya replies with a bit of guilt as he realizes he had again missed a number of calls from Tarjani post his unanticipated departure. He had however sent her a text, saying he would call her back soon.

'Now that you are sure about her, when are you getting her to meet us?' Her eagerness is clearly visible on her face.

'She has an event tomorrow…,' Agastya pauses before saying, 'maybe after that…' He feels a sudden emptiness. He now realizes how indifferently he had reacted to her when he had left from Guwahati. It bothers him. He knows that he has done something awful. He has to either get tougher or start listening to his conscience—this guilt does no good to anyone.

'What happened?' Addya questions him.

'Nothing! I think she has left for Delhi,' Agastya says, deep in thought.

'Why?' she asks, gesturing Agastya to sit on her bed.

'She was calling me and I could not receive her call. So, she contacted Arjun on Facebook and told him that she is coming to the hospital.'

'Then call her,' Addya tries to give him the solution. That is what she has always done. Agastya knows that the event was very important for Tarjani, but the fact that she didn't mind missing it for him makes him feel worse about himself. He realizes how selfish he has been. For a moment, he feels he does not deserve to be loved.

'Was my level of commitment enough to woo her when I was leaving? Definitely not,' he thinks. He has made her feel like he has dismissed her after spending a remarkable night with her. He feels uneasy inside, pauses, murmurs something to Addya that no one else can hear, and checks the earliest flight to Guwahati.

'You love her?' Addya asks him.

He nods.

'Then talk to her. I presume I am not in a position to advise you as I am already disillusioned with relationships. But I wish you all the best for your blooming love. I hope you make sufficient efforts to rekindle the magical relationship you have with her, a different yet similar to the kind that you have savoured and nurtured with me over the years. Do not ever make it complicated.'

Agastya turns and looks at Arjun.

'Thanks for taking care of her. It means a lot,' Agastya thanks him for everything.

'She is my sister too and this formality does not suit you. And listen, stop worrying all the time. Overthinking only creates problems that don't exist. You have to be strong, not worried,' Arjun tells him.

Agastya nods before her mother hands over a prescription to get some injections.

'What's that? I'll get it,' Arjun offers.

'You are just running around since yesterday. You sit and rest for some time. I will return in a few minutes.'

'Wait. I'll come with you,' says Arjun.

'Had I been a little more courageous to speak against the tide of opinions at the time of Addya's wedding, her life would have taken a different turn today. We had invited about

1,600 people to the grand wedding, probably a few more, and how many of them turned up during our troubled times? None,' Agastya's words convey the ugly truth.

'Forget the past, it remains unchanged. What really matters is that we have each other's back and that will remain constant,' Arjun assures him. He adds, 'I am not sure but I think you have time to make things work with Tarjani. So, all the best.' He takes the prescription from his hand.

'Are you sure?' Agastya asks him, holding a number of questions within.

'Yes, I would have done the same thing in this situation.'

Agastya books a ticket.

'I'll see you.' Agastya takes his bag and tells his mother that he needs to leave urgently. Arjun assures him that he will manage the rest. Agastya walks away with turbulence in his mind, and boards the next flight to Guwahati.

The climate is perfect—no torrent, no lightning, no rain, and the flight is ready to take off. Agastya stares at the screen repeatedly. When everything happens in the right order, it means that the order is not right. It makes him anxious.

Agastya drops Addya a message.

Please take care of yourself and the little one. I'll be back soon.

Addya replies instantly.

Yes. And I am curious to meet her:)

He drops another message to Tarjani.

When I become old, and am unable to go for a walk with you, when I have difficulty hearing and may not be able to see things, pictures we clicked will be of no use then. Do you know how I will remember our memories? I will close my eyes, and all the cute memories will come alive. It may sound cheesy, but I just wanted to say this.

And the flight takes off.

Agastya reaches the hotel in haste in the afternoon. His sight searches for the woman who had handed them the room key at the reception—Charvi.

'How can I help you, Sir?' the woman at the front desk asks him.

Agastya repeats the words Tarjani had said, 'I have an appointment with Mr Bharali, can you please check?' He adds, 'Is Charvi not on duty?'

'No sir, I am in charge,' she adds, 'I am sorry, Sir, but Mr Bharali has no meeting today. Can you provide your name, Sir?'

'Can you check his appointment with Tarjani?' Agastya requests.

'Yes, he had an appointment with Miss Tarjani for this afternoon but she cancelled the meeting at the last moment,' the woman responds.

'She had some medical emergency, so she has sent me on her behalf,' he acts to perfection. However, the lady questions, 'Do you have any document of representation on behalf of Miss Tarjani?'

'Yes, because it is an emergency, she cannot take calls

right now,' he shows his identity proof and the letter of representation that he forged at the last moment.

She responds with a fake smile, 'Okay Sir, please make yourself comfortable. Your meeting is in forty-five minutes.'

'So, I'll not get a room?' Agastya says in a hurry. He looks bothered and wants to settle down before he goes for the meeting.

'No Sir...'

Agastya responds before she can complete her sentence, 'Excuse me? No means...'

She responds faster than him, 'No Sir, I meant, this is your key card, enjoy your stay. And your breakfast timing is 7:30 a.m. to...'

Agastya checks his wristwatch and almost runs towards the lift, screaming, 'Thank you. Well, I am not going to be available for breakfast...'

Watching him run, the lady smiles to herself. Agastya calls Arjun before he gets ready to enter the conference room.

There are twenty-three people in the conference room. He has counted them. That is what he does in his corporate sessions. Some of the employees, perhaps assistants and interns, glance through the windows. Though speaking has been his bread and butter for quite some time, he feels a flutter in his stomach—as if butterflies are performing a ballet in the rain. Agastya studies the group. He feels extremely nervous. He opens his laptop and readies some pictures that Tarjani had shared with him during their late night conversations. It is easy to watch someone but difficult to get into their shoes.

He gulps a sip of water and clears his throat.

'Hello everyone,' he starts. 'I will not take much of your time. As people say, the one who works with his hands is a labourer. The one who works with his hands and his head is a craftsman, and the one who works with his hands, head and heart is an artist. Today, I am here on behalf of the founder of Uzaro. Unfortunately, she had to leave at the last moment due to some medical emergency, and I feel fortunate enough to represent the work of Uzaro. Going by the nomenclature, Uzaro means tiny smiles. As we all know, everyone is surrounded by thousands of stories. And if an artwork helps to find your story, then the artwork becomes alive. It breathes with you when you wake up in the morning. It listens to your story before you go to bed. It brings tiny smiles to your face. You can feel its intangible touch. It has a part of you in it, and you are yourself when you look at it.

'Now, coming to why we are here. Previously, hotels used to purchase luxurious art from companies who used to produce the same artwork in bulk. However, times are changing, and premium hotels want to now invest in unique artworks to create a lasting impact on their customers. We, at Uzaro, want to cater to this futuristic core need of hotels by providing unique handmade artworks that will help this hotel to not only have an impactful ambiance but also create a "wow" effect on our customers. Thank you,' says Agastya, displaying the pictures on the projector.

Every person in the room is smiling. They are smiles of respect and gratitude. With enthusiasm, the conference bursts into applause. Agastya welcomes the appreciation with gratification, which is evident in his smile. A member of the marketing teams asks him, 'Are you the marketing person for Uzaro?'

'Yes, I joined recently,' he smiles.

Mr Bharali, whom he wanted to impress probably more than he had wanted to meet Tarjani for the first time, congratulates him with a smile, asking when they could begin work.

He sends a text to Arjun.

Thank you for the write-up. Seems to have worked.

The screen flashes.

I hope it went well ☺

He cherishes their appreciative expressions, this time in his memory and not in any folder. He cannot wait to tell Tarjani about this eventful day. A successful relationship is about two people using their power and energy to help and uplift each other. Two people in a healthy relationship always complement and complete each other.

Thirteen

Agastya is delighted as he rushes to Room Number 1407 of the hospital to meet Addya. He knows Tarjani is also there, as Arjun had informed him of her arrival when he was at the Guwahati airport. He still has not told her the wonderful thing he has done to rectify things. Agastya knows what to do next to build a good connection between Tarjani and Addya. He grins to himself. He seems more relaxed now.

'Look who is here,' Addya announces in excitement, taking the support of the headrest of her bed. Agastya intends on making the rest of the evening special for Tarjani. He is already exhilarated at the mere thought of disclosing the news to her. Tarjani would have never come to Delhi if she did not have strong feelings for him. Agastya understands this when he looks into her eyes, which are full of love.

'Hey!' says Tarjani awkwardly.

'Hey, how are you?' Agastya steps closer to the sofa, where Arjun is sitting and examining the bills.

'I am good...' are the only words that come out of Tarjani.

Without saying anymore, he gives her the yellow envelope.

'What's this?' asks an agitated Tarjani. She does not know anything as Arjun is good at keeping secrets and has not mentioned anything to her. Addya stares at him in disbelief hoping this is not some sort of proposal. She sighs with relief that their mother is not around else she would question his maturity. Tarjani takes out the papers from the envelope. A smile creeps up on her face as she reads the content of the envelope, warming her skin like the rays of the summer sun.

'What the fu...' Tarjani struggles to speak. 'How did you do that?' She still cannot believe that he has done it. But Agastya would never play a prank of this sort.

'The late-night study sessions in college helped me realize that miracles can happen overnight,' he jokes. Her usual cautious grin explodes into a radiant smile that he has never seen before. It seems like everything is going to get better. She has Agastya, and he has her. Life is full of possibilities.

Suddenly, Agasyta spots something—an envelope on Addya's bed, peeping from under the pillow. He notices a local address that seems familiar to him.

'What's that?' questions Agastya.

Tough times don't last, tough people do. Heartbreaks are crucial; they strengthen us to face challenges in life. Addya had never had a relationship before she got married because she always dreamt of having a love story with the person she would get married to. Now, she can only feel the pain of a broken relationship.

Anger boils in Agastya like lava as he reads the divorce notice for Addya for the third time as it had been undelivered before. Bali is verbally claiming that the child is not his—adding to his inhumanity. Addya does not cry anymore because she has realized that it is not worth a moment of her time to be with a person who can say something like this. She never belonged to him, to that place. And when it comes to the issue of proving the child's paternity, it is just a test away. She is not worried, just ashamed at his monstrous act to shun his own child.

It is heart-wrenching that in our society people gossip about the girl who goes through such difficult situations but nobody has the courage to speak against the man who is the cause of it. That is the ugly truth of our society, which prides itself in being educated and intellectual.

Agastya had never thought that the one who had given him strength during difficult times would need his help and support in her tough times. He had never imagined that she would share her grief with him when she was supposed to share it with the person she was married to. The thought alone fills him with rage. Agastya needs to find other comforting words than 'never give up' because she has already given up her self-respect to fix things after getting married, in order to make everyone happy. But she has failed miserably.

Within him churns a hunger for destruction, and Agastya knows it is too much for him to handle. The pressure of this raging sea of anger forces him to say things, and he wants to express what he has been suppressing for months. He knows that this feeling will not pass until he does what he wants to. So, he escapes. He runs.

'I'll be back in sometime.'

'Where are you going?' asks Addya.

'Need to go somewhere. It is important. Please call me if you need anything.'

The door closes.

Arjun approaches Addya to inquire about the call she had received from an unknown number. She tells him that she had received several rape threats in a day, which was a sickening reminder of the devastating consequence of raising her voice. That is how women are secured in this 'empowered' society.

'Did you inform the police?' Arjun asks her. He has always encouraged Addya to settle things without going into legal battles, but now he is too worried for her.

'I informed the local police station, but the lady constable dismissed it by saying, "I also get these types of threat calls. No need to worry about it,"' saying this, Addya smiles, which depicts her helplessness. Arjun is in deep thought, trying to think about the best possible solution.

Meanwhile, Agastya ends up in Bali's home. He rushes inside with fury and hatred oozing out of his narrowed eyes and stony expression. Even before the gates are opened completely, he pushes the gate hard and barges inside. Bali tries to check who is at the gate. He remains silent and looks at Agastya with disgust. Agastya holds his collar and looks into his frightened eyes, 'If you do not stop messing around with my family, then you are going to die right here in your house. You have ruined my sister's life, and I will ruin yours, got it? Maybe you do not know me well. I am fucking insane when it comes to my family. So, you and your vicious father better be in your limits. I am not afraid of you and I am also ready to face the consequences, but I am sure, you and your family are not. I will separate your arms and legs, and boil them until they become jelly. I will then throw it in the river. No one will find your bodies. Stay away.'

Agastya does not look as vulnerable as he feels, and knows that if he does not control his emotions, he will create more problems for Addya and weaken her case. His words make Bali and his father squirm. He can be very dangerous to anyone, and so, at the moment no one follows him as he storms out of Bali's house.

> Agastya, why are you not picking up my call? Where are you?

The cellphone lights up with a message from Tarjani. He swipes left and reaches the hospital as quickly as he can. A lot has happened in an hour. However, after giving it a serious thought, Agastya is ready to face the consequences.

At the hospital, Agastya opens the window and lets the evening air come in. Addya's eyes dart towards the window and she sees a bare tree branch silently swaying in the evening breeze. Replacing her thumb with a bookmark, Addya shuts the book that Arjun has given her, which she has been reading since yesterday.

'This guy knows how to sell books,' Addya teases Arjun while Tarjani fiddles with her phone. Her mother is reading the newspaper.

'Definitely, he does,' Tarjani adds. She remembers her conversation with Agastya at the airport when he was telling her how Arjun had promoted his books.

'Brothers be like...' Agastya chuckles, and Arjun smiles.

Though Tarjani and Arjun have not spent much time together, they share a cordial bond.

'Agastya, you need to drop Tarjani to the airport, don't you?' questions Addya, and then continues looking at Tarjani, 'Wait, I'll book a cab for you.'

Arjun tells Agastya, who appears to be wearing a jacket and putting on his shoes, 'Agastya can drop her. He has some work at home, so he can drop her on the way.'

'Yes, we can go,' Tarjani says, 'I think it is the same route,' she looks at Agastya and nods in agreement.

'And I'll get your stuff from home while coming back,' Agastya tells his mother.

'Take care of yourself, don't stress yourself with work,' his mother hugs Tarjani. The hug feels like home to Tarjani.

'Thanks, Aunty. Come to Lucknow sometime, we would love to show you the city,' Tarjani offers.

'We will,' Agastya's mother assures her and adds, ' And I am sorry I couldn't treat you well here.'

'No formalities at all, Aunty. I completely understand,' she hugs her again.

'Okay, thanks for coming,' says Addya, waving goodbye.

'Now I just want you to be fit and fine, and then I'll come again,' Tarjani approaches Addya and hugs her tightly. Then, she takes her backpack and handbag and walks out of the door. Agastya takes the car keys and they depart.

'Why so silent?' Tarjani enquires in the car when Agastya gives her a look.

'Nothing,' says Agastya. Before Tarjani can question further, Agastya changes his expressions to look casual—as if nothing has happened.

'No. Tell me, what happened?' repeats Tarjani.

'Arjun knows that I am taking you home,' Agastya changes the topic.

'Does he?' asks Tarjani.

'Rather, he only suggested.'

Parents may not agree, but it is okay to spend quality time with the one you plan to spend the rest of your life with rather than regretting it later. If Addya could have spent a little more time with Bali, she would have seen his true colours. Though Agastya hasn't proposed marriage to Tarjani yet, this is the right time to get to know her.

It is a myth that love is just about two people. No, a true marriage—and true love—is never about just you. It is about the person you love—their desires, their needs, their aspirations, and their thoughts. Self-indulgence demands, 'What's in it for me?', while love asks, 'What can I give?'

'I guessed that but was not sure,' she locks her long fingers with his on the gear. Agastya looks into her sensual eyes, and an unfamiliar feeling arouses in him. 'Love you,' he says. Eyes can speak volumes without uttering a single word.

'Always,' says Tarjani.

'I want to show you my place,' Agastya says in excitement.

Tarjani has a flight to board at night, and Agastya wishes to spend some time with her before that.

Fourteen

They reach Agastya's house. He knows that the neighbourhood aunties will shoot myriad questions at him regarding Addya's well-being. He is devising ways to escape the clutches of these ever-so-intrigued women.

'Should I take your bag?' Agastya asks as Tarjani looks a little tired and shaky. She has not slept peacefully since the last few days, in the midst of all the running around.

'No, I am fine,' she tiptoes on the stairs, discussing more about how Agastya cracked the deal and impressed Mr Bharali with his words. When they reach the first floor where Agastya lives with his family, he unlocks the door. He does not want the neighbours to know about Tarjani's arrival. She peeps vigilantly and finds the next-door neighbour closing the door. Agastya enters the house quickly and shuts the door behind them in haste. He also draws the curtains because he knows Delhiites love to hold long-distance conversation from their balconies.

'Let's go there and switch off the lights here. This is directly visible from outside, and I do not want my mother to know about you from them,' he points at a giant sliding window, which can easily be viewed from the other side of the neighbourhood.

She chuckles, 'No problem. I understand. Well, this is a nice peaceful place to live in.'

As she strolls around the house, she glances into a room. Tarjani finds notebooks on the table, along with a few make-up things like lip gloss, eyeliner and an undergarment in the corner, that he quickly hides behind his back and chucks into the laundry basket.

'That's okay. I am not spying. Your room is probably cleaner than mine. My place smells of paint all the time,' says Tarjani as she studies the place.

'This is Addya's room as she needs fresh air from the balcony. And I don't want to change your perception about myself by inviting you to my room. It's a mess,' he says and takes her to the balcony.

'Oh! Was this already planned without my knowledge?' Tarjani asks him coyly. There is a sofa in the balcony, with a bottle of wine and a pair of glasses. It is a little dark outside, but they can see each other.

'Perhaps,' he mutters.

'Who did that? Arjun?' questions Tarjani as she sits on the sofa in the balcony, resting her chin on her knees and wrapping her hands around her legs.

Agastya nods and asks, 'You want something to eat?'

In the candlelit balcony, with soft sensual music playing in the hall and a bottle of red wine, the evening feels very romantic.

'Woah, never thought you had a romantic side. Quite interesting,' she says, nodding her head dramatically.

Agastya sits closer to her. 'Don't make that face,' he looks at her and grins.

He pours wine in the glasses and gives one to her.

'Okay. Thanks,' she smiles and holds the glass.

'You know what? Whenever I feel sad and discouraged, I come here and sit in the balcony. It brings me peace,' he says as he holds her hand.

'Thank you for everything,' Tarjani repeats with more affection.

'You are welcome! Moreover, that was all your hard work, I just showed them your art,' he says and smiles.

♥

'Just give me a minute,' Agastya remarks, going inside the kitchen. He brings out a plate of chocolate loaf that Arjun had baked when he was home the previous day.

'Oh my god... You made this?' Tarjani sets aside her glass and takes the plate delightfully. 'Oh, you're a chef! Both Arjun and you are quite similar, aren't you?' she exclaims.

'Probably, because we both have spent enough time in the kitchen with our mothers,' Agastya laughs, excited to hear appreciation.

When he notices that Tarjani is still surprised, Agastya nods and says, 'Well, not many skills are required for this. Arjun had made this for Addya to help her with her craving.'

They sit close to each other and share an intimate conversation. When you sincerely love someone, you want that person to stay in your life and you start thinking of every possible way to stay together. You sense that strong desire in yourself. It feels like an obsession. This is the kind of obsession they have developed for each other and it is visible in their acts of love and care for each other. Agastya makes efforts to make her feel special. After all, no relationship is all sunshine and no rain—it depends on how quickly you fix things before they become rotten. That is important.

♥

'Well, this is amazing,' Tarjani responds after a long silence. She is looking at the hanging wind chimes when a sudden gust of breeze hits them.

'Thank you,' Agastya says and checks his wristwatch. It seems like he is trying to tell Tarjani something.

'Is anything bothering you?' Tarjani figures out that something is wrong from his expression.

'I have been trying to perfect this to present it to you, but it is nowhere around what I wanted to create,' Agastya presents her a unique artwork, similar to the piece Agastya saw at Uzaro for the first time. However, the special thing about this artwork is that it contains a picture of both of them from college.

Tarjani is overwhelmed and holds it as if it is the most fragile thing. She takes the wrapped box, opens it in excitement, and looks quietly at the artwork Agastya has tried to create from whatever he has understood and seen while working with her. The A4-sized frame has an old picture of Tarjani in focus and Agastya is in the background—it was taken during the college farewell.

'God, you have put in so much effort. This looks amazing,' her eyes glitter.

'Yes, and it is safe. Even if you put it in the gallery, no one will ever want to buy it,' he laughs without worrying about how bad it looks. For now, only their emotions matter.

She beams, 'I like this. This was during college farewell.'

And then, she adds, 'Before you invest more time in gifts and do out-of-the-box things intentionally or unintentionally, I would like to ask, what if, I want to marry you. I mean, will you marry me?' Tarjani says all this as if she has prepared it—precise and accurate. She adds, 'Because you took years and couldn't even say that you had a crush on me, I have to take this initiative.'

He gets up and hugs her tightly. They stand silently like that for a few minutes. Agastya kisses her on her forehead. They both know that they are no longer alone in the journey of life. Agastya holds Tarjani in his arms, and they kiss passionately. He kisses her, once, twice, thrice, until he can taste her lips, and realizes he will never have enough of them.

Why does everything feel surreal when people are in the midst of a whirlwind of emotions? Agastya did not expect this and is thrilled. Tarjani waves her hand in front of him and breaks his reverie. She asks, 'Hey, what happened to you? What are you thinking?'

Agastya remains silent. He cannot say anything as he is almost choking with emotions.

'Nothing,' he manages to reply.

'Not again, Agastya!' she exclaims, confused if it is her proposal or something about Addya that is agitating him.

'I think I only pretend to be okay in front of people when everyone asks about Addya. In reality, I am not! I am helpless when it comes to expressing my feelings. Before I say anything, I think so much and so many things but often I barely have anything to speak, and simply listen to people rambling. That makes me feel introverted and abandoned. And I am always terrified of losing important things in life,' Agastya begins to voice the unsaid words in his mind. That is how special their bond is.

'Everything is overwhelming right now. I wrote something for Addya on her birthday but I did not give it to her. I do not know what is wrong. I think I am unable to salvage situations.' Agastya pauses for a minute and finds himself sharing something he has been suppressing, 'I went to his place alone and warned him. If Addya or Mom comes to know, they will start hiding things from me. I already know they do. It will only worsen with time.'

This stunned Tarjani. Now, she understands the gravity of the situation and how things can worsen if the right measures are not taken.

'What? Did you go to Bali's place?' a shocked Tarjani asks him.

Agastya nods.

'Why did you do that? They can file a complaint against you for threatening them. Do you realize how much potential it has to weaken Addya's case? Aunty was telling me she is afraid to tell you everything because you become aggressive. Listen! Doing this is the last option. Control your anger, and use it at the right time.' Tarjani understands how this misdemeanour can ricochet for him and his family.

She adds, 'Now that it is done, there is no point thinking about it. However, you must think of the future,' and suggests discussing it with Arjun. She thinks Arjun can take wise decisions in this situation.

'I don't know but my mind starts coming up with unwanted thoughts and mental images that I know can be harmful or violent, either to myself or to others. I am trying to fix this,' says Agastya.

Tarjani envelops Agastya tightly in her arms—providing the warmth and calmness he needs. She whispers, 'You don't have to fix your whole life right now, you just have to try and not give up.'

A crying man becomes the strongest if he has someone to wipe his tears in his life. This unquestionably helps him feel stronger and not alone anymore. Almost all the problems in life can be solved with courage, belief and patience. That is what Tarjani encourages him to do in this difficult phase of life. Tarjani buries her face in his neck and Agastya laughs when Tarjani quickly tickles him.

'Let's pack, we need to reach the airport on time,' says Agastya, releasing himself with a quick kiss. He books a cab to the airport.

♥

One must strive to learn two things, first, see what is important to you, prioritize it, and second, ignore the rest of the world until you fulfil your priority. However, in such situations, Agastya does not even know what to prioritize and what to ignore.

'Why don't we engage Addya with something that she likes? That is the most important thing for her at this point. She is going through a difficult time, and she has Takshika to take care of. She can come to Lucknow if she wishes to, I am sure, she would love it there,' Tarjani leaves the question for Agastya to ponder over as he drives her to the airport. Agastya nods.

'And please do not do anything that will weaken your case in the hearing,' Tarjani does not wish to remind him of the gruesome encounter with Bali because it disturbs him; Agastya needs emotional support after what he has initiated without anyone's consent.

'You will get late, and we will talk about this once you reach home.' They both walk to the entry gate, and she waves back. She reaches the airport at the nick of time. Moving quickly, she gets her boarding pass and walks towards the assigned boarding gate.

Fifteen

Addya's mother is still contemplating whether to pursue the claim in the court or to attempt to resolve the dispute without taking any legal action. Damage to one's reputation is often an unexpected cost of legal action. People gossip endlessly, until the woman succeeds in getting her rights.

Addya's family finally decide to pursue the case legally when Bali sends them a legal notice and one cannot ignore a hearing in the court. The previous hearings did not go in Addya's favour when they were absent from the court, and so their presence becomes necessary. It is sad that Addya has to dress according to the dress code of the court when she has bigger things to worry about in life—like a month-and-a-half-old baby.

Addya finds the courtroom suffocating. It appears dingy and has a squalid surrounding. With the sheer number of documents and applications filed by lawyers every day, the courtroom is littered with stacks of papers all around. There are no separate desks for the two sides. Instead, there is one long desk with two small podiums for lawyers to use for their briefs. While the man at the door is chewing tobacco and peeking from the corner of the walls, the families seated on the front bench, who took a vow to stand by each other in happiness and sorrow, are today standing against each other.

There are a few people who are just sitting in the pew, watching the proceedings, and many lawyers, who are patiently waiting for their cases to be called out. There are times when personal questions are asked in the court, often leading to people laughing hysterically. Addya had requested her lawyer to proceed with the case only in the presence of both the parties, not publicly. The lawyer had appealed but the judge had rejected the plea on the basis of the fact that it was not mentioned in the law, and only special cases were held under CCTV surveillance, and for other cases, the public could attend the proceedings. The judge believes that it is important to spread awareness and reduce crime. Giving this explanation, the lawyer proceeds. The clerk enters and looks at the wall clock in the room. Then, he sits at his table to review files and maintain day-to-day records of court proceedings.

♥

'Case number 121,' the man standing at the gate shouts in a rough voice. Two more people are sitting next to the judge. The judge examines the file and looking at the lawyers, announces, 'Yes, please proceed with the case.'

The accused group of people, in this case, were travelling in the handicapped compartment of a train. 'Do you all plead guilty?' the judge asks.

The officer who brought the group looks at them and murmurs, 'Say, yes we do.'

'Yes, we do,' the group says.

'Okay, charge them a penalty of ₹500 each and set them free,' he says.

'Don't do this again,' he adds.

The officer then escorts them to the exit, saying, 'Move. Move.'

He starts collecting the penalty from them, and then a young man from the group says, 'Sir, will I get the receipt?'

The man almost shouts, 'If you want the receipt, you have to wait for two hours. Why are you wasting time here? Go to work. Do not travel again in the handicapped compartment.'

Then, the man announces, 'Case number 122.'

♥

Both the lawyers stand up and take permission to proceed.

'As you may already know the case, I would also like to bring something to the kind attention of the honourable court. It is no coincidence that the plaintiff and his family had installed CCTV cameras in their home just before their wedding. They always compelled my client to talk within the purview of the cameras to falsely hold her culpable of wrongdoing. In addition, she is wrongly accused of torturing the plaintiff and his family.'

'I kindly request the court to review these inferences critically in the light of sufficient and appropriate testaments that have been provided. These inferences seem highly misleading and speculative. My client tried her best to maintain a healthy decorum with the plaintiff, and his family. We have received confirmation of this from his immediate neighbour who once noticed an offence against my client.

'I would also like to draw your kind attention to the fact that my client resigned from her job as an esteemed professor and furthermore, terminated her classes in the best interests of her family. That's it, Your Honour,' finishes Mr Bhardwaj, Addya's lawyer.

Mr Rastogi, the plaintiff's lawyer, rises immediately, requesting, 'I call Mrs Addya to the dock. I want to ask her a few questions. Do I have the permission, My Lord?'

'Permission granted.'

'Yes, please,' Addya says in a quiet voice; barely anyone can hear her. The crowd leans in, scooting to the edge of their seats. The lawyer seems in favour of her in the way he talks and smiles at her. That is how lawyers are. He proceeds, 'So when did you stop giving private tuitions? Did you return their fees? If yes, how did you return the amount?'

'Your Honour, Mr Rastogi is trying to lead my client.'

'No, it's okay. It's okay, sir. I want to answer,' Addya looks at her lawyer reassuringly and continues, 'I never took advance from my students. Neither was it a private tuition. There were seven students including three female students. All of them were asked to show their identity proofs because my in-laws doubted my character.'

'Do you have any other question?' the judge asks the plaintiff lawyer and then asks the defendant lawyer the same question.

'Your Honour, the fact remains that my client started feeling unsafe in their home. So, she left her home while she was one-month pregnant. Also, the plaintiff and his family are openly endorsing and encouraging an act which is an offence under Section 304B and Section 498A. The plaintiff and his family constantly tortured her. My client was harassed for dowry by her in-laws from the very next day of her marriage. She was also physically assaulted by the accused and his family. Unfortunately, there is no strict law for marital rape under the Indian Penal Code. Multiple cases are reported where women in our society have to bear the brunt due to the lack of legitimacy of law enforcement and people like Mr Bali get away with malicious acts. The plaintiff is accused of forcing my client for sex on a regular basis, and when she refused, he resorted to coercive means and began to defame her. I request you to consider her appeal and her future with her newborn baby. That is it, Your Honour. Thank you.'

'I object, My Lord. My client has been wrongly accused of demanding dowry. He is innocent. With regards to the physical assault, they just had a verbal fight on a trivial domestic issue,' Mr Rastogi argues.

'I object, Your Honour. They just had a petty argument and she got seriously injured? Isn't that astonishing?' cuts in Addya's lawyer, Mr Bhardwaj.

'No! That's absolutely untrue,' says Mr Rastogi.

'Order! Order! Both the lawyers settle down and maintain the decorum of the court,' demands the judge.

'Sir, we request you to grant us the next date as I have a witness who is currently unwell and suffering from dengue. The doctors have asked him to take rest, the recovery of which will take over a month,' the plaintiff's lawyer requests the judge.

'Okay, next date, 22 November.'

It is a well-known tactic to ask for the next date when there is nothing to provide as evidence in the present. But the judge still grants them another date. Agastya recalls that the lawyer did not state that he went to threaten Bali. That worries him more as he fears they have some secret weapon against Addya or him.

♥

'Don't worry, if they are not able to defend themselves for a few more months, we will win the case due to lack of opposition,' the lawyer says.

'Uncle, it's awkward when they ask such questions in public. Last time, too, the police officer was treating me as if I have already lost the case,' Addya almost cries.

'You have to be the strongest right now, okay? We had appealed to have the session only between the parties, but it has been rejected. You will rarely see the people who attended your wedding ceremony. These are unknown faces, so there is no point feeling awkward. Don't worry about it,' he says, explaining everything logically.

♥

'Can we fight the case from any other city?' Agastya asks out of curiosity. Addya nods in agreement.

'Irrespective of the location, the material facts and testimonies remain unchanged. Our case is not special to get us any privileges, so as I said, you have to be the strongest,' the lawyer tries to make the family understand.

'No, I am saying, can I transfer my case to the Mumbai session court? I am shifting to my cousin's place in Mumbai. Because Bali's father has served here in this court for several years, he might be able to change things. 'He may fight Bali's case using his influence and expose Addya to questions that she may not be able to answer,' Agastya remarks.

Addya has not thought about it and is unsure about the move, but Arjun has advised Agastya to bring Addya to Mumbai and fight the case there. He believes that this way things will be easier for her. Arjun is acquainted with some notable lawyers, and according to the law, Addya has the right to demand a transfer of this sort. There may be challenges but that will remain inevitable for both the parties. Agastya insists the lawyer to consider the plea.

'I'll have to check on that. I am not very sure, but there have been situations where cases were shifted. When are you planning to shift? Please let me know the dates in advance,' says the lawyer.

'We have a month's time to weigh all the possibilities,' Agastya declares.

'I am pissed off about getting another date every time,' Addya murmurs. His mother tries to comfort her. Agastya takes everyone home after a hectic day.

Addya's lawyer prepares to file a petition for the case to be shifted outside Delhi as his client is apprehensive about a fair trial and her safety.

Sixteen

'Can you come here for a minute? I need your help,' sprawled on her bed, Addya yells from her room to call her mother.

'What happened?' Agastya enters instead. Her mom responds from the other room, 'Just give me fifteen minutes.'

'Chill, it is nothing,' Addya responds.

'When did you become a bookworm?' asks Agastya, amused.

With a long-drawn yawn, she shows him some designs that Tarjani had sketched during her visit to the hospital. She says, 'Not a bookworm. I was checking this out. You like them?'

'They are nice,' he takes the sketch pad from her hand and notices the sketches on the last page.

'Tarjani was explaining to me the basics of a composition before it turns into reality.'

The bed creaks as Agastya sits beside her. He says, 'You need to get back to work soon. I know you miss it.'

'I desperately want to...' she pauses and asks Agastya for help, 'but for now, could you help me clean the baby? Or just hold her. This human being is not even thirty centimetres, does not speak, but cries and screams all the time, and poops whenever she feels like.'

'Sure.'

'Do you have any idea how to do it?' Addya jests.

'This is no rocket science... Come here,' says Agastya.

Agastya positions himself on the bed. He takes a packet of medical gloves and tears it open.

Addya laughs, 'God! Why gloves?'

'Listen! I am just avoiding any infection to the baby,' Agastya gently removes the diaper and cleans with fresh wipes. Then, he extends another one to Addya.

'Okay! Okay! I think, you are better than Mom,' she teases and continues, 'you can replace her.'

'Definitely not,' he pokes her.

'Ouch! Careful, you idiot.'

'Well, once you are back to work, you should think of doing something of your own. You always wanted to, right? Why don't you work with Tarjani? She is planning to expand her work to Mumbai. I am very sure she will. So, I can plan something for you in Mumbai. I will discuss this with Tarjani. Also, let us talk to Arjun. I assume you both will have a good bond if you spend time in a 10 × 10 room. You should think more about framing your future rather than being stabbed in the present by the remnants of your past.'

'I am just trying to get an edge to start things afresh. I am not sure about anything. Sometimes I feel I should not have let my child come into this world. I could have stopped...,' says Addya.

Before she can make more remarks that could sully her thoughts against her child because of the situation she is in, Agastya interrupts her, 'There is absolutely no need to curse your child... I would be glad to take care of her if you can't. So, stop overthinking.'

'I didn't mean it. I am sorry,' Addya realizes the enormity of her words.

'Well, we all are there to help you. We do not know anything about what we have been exposed to, so you cannot expect us to be perfect from the first day. It may take days or years to be the mother you want to be, but you cannot stop trying,' Agastya tries to keep her away from any negativity.

'Now I see why you're so good at your job,' Addya wishes she could help him instead of always taking his help.

Agastya sits back on the bed and looks at her earnestly. He knows one thing—whether she plans to shift to Mumbai or not, she needs to free herself from overthinking and trauma.

Agastya suggests that she relocates while their mother can take care of Takshika and he can regularly visit them, on and off, just to keep a check on the little princess's welfare. He knows that she won't agree to it but Agastya needs to convince her by any means. He believes that relocation and work appointment documents will help strengthen their case as well.

'Are you sure it will help us? Our lawyer has already said that things will remain the same everywhere,' Addya seems unsure about this arrangement. Mumbai will be an entirely new place for her.

'You need a change of scene,' he suggests.

'I am not too sure about this, Agastya.'

'You need some fresh air and you need to get out of your own head,' says Agastya.

Seventeen

'Have you packed everything?' Her emotional mother asks Addya, entering her room.

Addya is looking at her daughter and is trying to hold back her tears. That is what mothers do. They both are experiencing similar feelings of despondence at the thought of leaving their child.

'Yes,' she says and adds, 'I am taking her with me. I'll manage.' Her emotions will not allow her to keep her child away from herself.

'It will be difficult for you to manage alone. I can take care of her here. You go and finish your work,' says her mother.

'I'll manage and Agastya is also coming along,' Addya starts packing the little one's clothes and other things before her mother takes her into her arms.

'Are you sure?' she asks her again.

'Completely,' Addya assures.

'Okay, keep your medicines, take care of yourself.' She looks at her for a response. She knows Arjun will take good care of her.

'And stay positive,' saying this, she takes her stuff from her hand.

'That's hard but I'll try my best.'

'Hard? Addya, you have survived horrible days with a monstrous man, dealt with recurring pre-delivery pregnancy issues, and now you are leaving your home for an entirely new place; you've just been released from the hospital. Nothing can get more gruelling than this. You are a fighter. Fight your way out, all right?' her mother encourages her.

Her mother is more worried because she has found sleeping pills in her medical kit. Addya had consumed those pills when she was pregnant. Agastya is unaware of this.

'I don't know what the future holds for you, but just don't take stress, Addya,' she says.

'Yes, Mom. It is going to be okay. I just want to get rid of this unnecessary background noise playing in my head,' Addya says.

Whenever she is alone, she starts thinking about her past and that makes her uneasy. There are so many memories, including the happy ones. Yet the troubled ones take precedence, along with negative sentiments. She reminisces about her past, the impediments that seem to have gripped her life. She has handled them fearlessly but she is tired now—tired of faking a smile, when all she wants to do is scream and vent all of her frustration. 'Everyone pretends. Sometimes to others, sometimes to themselves,' Addya tells herself. Then, she says, 'Mom, you just stay away from irrelevant gossip and take good care of yourself.'

'No one is gossiping, Addya, your uncles care for you,' her mother is trying to be strong and Addya knows it. But she wants her to stay away from pretentious people. Many of them do not even care enough to pretend.

'I don't think so. Aren't those the same people who encouraged my father to not send me abroad even after

I received a scholarship? Let us not get into that. You and dad always wanted me to be happy, so I will try to be. I just need some time. You take care of yourself,' Addya packs everything into a bag and embraces her mother warmly. Agastya enters the room—just the right person she does not wish to discuss all the wrong things with. She can never predict the things he might do in a fit of rage.

'This is the time to concentrate on your life. Remember one thing, Addya, the slightest of execution is worth more than millions of intentions,' Agastya prompts. He rechecks the ticket and keeps a copy of it in each of their bags.

'Did you keep warm clothes?' her mother checks with Addya and Agastya.

'Weather is normal over there, I had checked with Arjun yesterday,' replies Agastya.

'Well, finish packing and then sleep.' Her mother comes out with Agastya and tells him, 'Be with her.'

'I'll take some trips back home in the upcoming weeks but she will be fine. Don't worry,' Agastya keeps a hand on her shoulder and nods. It is enough for her. That is how much she trusts him.

While gazing out of the window of the plane, Addya is holding her baby in her arms and sniffling. When she notices Agastya's vigilant eyes on her, she refuses to make any eye contact with him for she is afraid of breaking down. She continues reading the book that Arjun had given her when she was in the hospital.

'Are you okay?' Agastya asks her.

Addya smiles and responds, 'Yeah, I am fine.'

She turns the first page of the book, pretending to read while her mind drifts through painful thoughts. With moist eyes, she reads the book and falls asleep before Agastya wraps a stole around her and quietly takes the book from her hand.

♥

Sometimes, words from our own people are more impactful than what we read. Sometimes it is the opposite. That is why letters are always precious. Agastya knows that words should only be spoken when they are required and they become precious when shared at the right moment with the right person. Agastya takes his pen and writes something on the last blank page of the book Addya was reading. He closes the book, puts it in her bag, reclines his seat, and closes his eyes until they reach Mumbai.

The perfect pot is the one that the potter gives a perfect shape to, not only from the outside but from the inside as well. Agastya knows this and that is what he tries to do with people who interact with him—that is what he is doing with his sister. He wants to make her believe that things are going to be okay in the end.

Eighteen

*D*rowsy and lethargic, Arjun briskly runs his hand through his hair and draws the curtains. He goes to the balcony and basks in the vibrant sunshine. But he does not have the time to stretch and enjoy the morning view. He has to receive Addya and Agastya. For that, he has to reach the airport on time.

'Where there is a will, there is a way' is an old maxim, the new one in his life being 'When there is a problem, there is Dimpy Aunty.' He calls her.

'Good morning,' wishes Arjun.

'Good morning! So Addya and Agastya have reached home? When are you bringing them here?' she shoots questions at him. Dimpy Aunty is equally excited to meet them. She had been excited to meet Arjun's mother as well but Arjun never wanted both of them to meet. The one time they had met, they had tried to dig everything out of his life—even things that were not meant to be discussed or addressed.

'Their flight got delayed, but the problem is a little bigger,' Arjun does not know how to clean the mess he and his friends, Sudeep and Ved, created last night. Arjun and Ved have been living together for almost a year now.

Arjun, Anushka and Ved had studied in the same college. They had both come to Mumbai as engineers, but Ved couldn't keep up with his job. He had not wanted to keep up with them either. They had been good friends in college, but after college, everyone got busy with their lives. They had not been in touch for several years. A few years ago, when Ved had started looking for a place to live, Arjun had landed up in Mumbai. Anushka had happened to know that they both were looking for a home and had suggested that they move in together.

Arjun tells Dimpy Aunty, 'Can you drive me to the airport in an hour?'

'I wish I could, but I have cramps. So, I will send the driver? My legs are cramped, but my hands are perfectly fine. I am making a nice lunch, so bring them here,' she says.

'Hmm. Okay,' says Arjun, checking the call log.

'What happened?'

His voice makes her conscious, and she asks again, 'What happened?'

'I got a call from an unknown number, and the man tried to threaten me after I put up a post on Instagram about Addya and the tough time she is going through. He was asking strange things and did not reveal his identity. And then, the same happened with Agastya, so, that concerns me more.'

'What? Did you call the police?' Dimpy Aunty asks.

'No, not yet, but I will,' Arjun assures her.

'This is bullshit. Wait, I will tell my husband. He has friends in Mumbai Police. Go with him and file a complaint. They will help you.'

Dimpy Aunty tells Arjun to take care of himself and instructs him to ask for any help if needed. Her husband has spent years in Mumbai, and he knows many authorities in Mumbai Cyber Cell. Over the years, Arjun has been threatened so often that he has become indifferent now. He is not afraid of them. He believes that it is the best part of his writing.

'Yes, I'll go. If I need any help, I will call uncle. Addya also received a few calls from different numbers, including rape threats.'

'Arjun, this is not steering in the right direction,' Dimpy Aunty says, worried.

'I know. She has informed the local police,' Arjun responds.

'Don't worry, we'll do something. For now, bring Addya here for lunch, and I will talk to her. Take care of yourself,' says Dimpy Aunty. Arjun can perceive the love and concern in her voice.

'Okay.'

As soon as the call disconnects, Ved surrounds him, 'Why did you not tell me?'

'It just happened yesterday evening, and then Sudeep was also at home, so I didn't get a chance,' Arjun justifies.

'Don't worry. Just give me that number. Let me call or, if needed, give me the address. I have friends in Delhi who can teach them a good lesson. If they are goons, I can show them what goons really mean,' Ved says violently, and takes out his phone, scrolling for a number in his call list.

'That is not required right now,' Arjun explains to Ved before he gets anxious. 'For now, what is important is to pick Addya and Agastya from the airport, and you need to help me organize the house before they arrive.'

♥

Addya rings the bell. Arjun is holding the baby in a handmade baby carrier against his chest that goes over his shoulder. Arjun rearranges his outfit and sets his hair again.

'Oh my goodness, the kind man at the door. Please come. It's great that you have come to meet us,' Dimpy Aunty welcomes them.

'Hi,' Arjun greets her by touching her knees.

'Aunty, this is Addya,' Arjun introduces her as if they do not know each other. 'Addya, she is the one you have heard many things about,' Arjun winks at Dimpy Aunty.

'We are already Instagram friends,' Dimpy Aunty laughs and continues, 'How are you, beta?' She gives Addya a warm hug.

'I am good, Aunty,'

She looks at Agastya. 'Glad to meet you. Please come.'

The door closes.

Arjun notices that things have changed at Anushka's home since he was last there. Anushka appears. Wearing a grimy housedress, she sits on the couch. Anushka looks like a typical Punjabi girl. Her natural jet-black unkempt hair curls around her forehead. She looks rather cute with a reluctant smile. Her lips are pink, always ready to curve into a smile. She has the perfect curves. At five feet four inches, with beautiful eyes and red cheeks, her soft and flawless skin has a natural glow, almost radiating positive energy. That is how Arjun would describe her.

Dimpy Aunty is cheerful but calm. She has a loving husband who spends most of his time with her, but these days, he is mostly travelling for work.

'Hey,' says Arjun to Anushka.

'Hello, how are you? Come,' she welcomes everyone gracefully, asking them to sit.

'A very positive place,' Addya looks around and sits on the sofa.

'By the way, Arjun, are you contesting to be the perfect man? I check out your kitchen activities on Instagram, and now, I am happy to see you becoming comfortable with the baby carrier,' Dimpy Aunty teases Arjun mercilessly.

'Has barbecuing been your hobby for years or did you just develop it after meeting me?' asks Arjun sarcastically.

'I think it happened after meeting you,' others join Dimpy Aunty as she laughs loudly.

They argue relentlessly, but both end up with smiling faces. Often in life, we meet people for no purpose. We meet, and we talk because that makes our hearts feel light and lively. Arjun has spent his most challenging time with her, and he knows that you should always stand by the person who has been with you in your worst times. Addya feels a completely different vibe around herself when she is with Dimpy Aunty.

Suddenly, Arjun starts laughing, looking at a tattoo of a wasp on Dimpy Aunty's neck.

'Don't laugh, I wanted this since college days but my father never allowed me to have one. So, I went ahead and fulfilled my wish.'

'Well, what to say,' Arjun grins.

♥

They sit around the dining table waiting for Anushka to serve the exotic home-cooked meal.

'I can help you,' Arjun peeks in the kitchen.

'I don't need you to. You will cook with me, and then you will post the picture on Instagram bagging all the credit for yourself. So, you sit and talk. I will be back in a moment,' Anushka rejects Arjun's offer.

'Okay. Okay,' Arjun laughs, returning to the hall.

'Listen!' shouts Anushka.

'Yeah,' Arjun turns and walks back into the kitchen.

'How are things with Addya?' she asks with a confused expression.

'Nothing, she is hopping from one court date to the next. Let's see when she comes out of all this. Once things are a bit settled, she can peacefully chase her aspirations.'

Arjun thinks of Agastya's situation, and what his family is going through.

'Let me know if I can be of any help to Addya or Agastya. I feel bad for her,' she says.

'She is smart, and she will figure something out for herself. We just want her to come out of this shit. That's it,' Arjun assures her.

'Does Mamma know about this?'

'Of course, look, it seems like she is already on duty.'

They look out into the hall where Dimpy Aunty is speaking to Addya and Agastya like long-lost friends uniting. She is fascinated by Agastya's work as a corporate trainer. She thinks it is one of the greatest jobs to motivate people about work-life balance.

'So how did you get this job?' she is more curious about Agastya and his work, shifting her attention from Arjun to him.

'Actually, it just happened. I did not aspire to be a trainer or a tutor. Initially, I was not interested in it, and then, I realized that there are more depressed souls than happy ones. That is why I began this journey of restoration of the lost souls.'

'And you enjoy it, that's more important,' states Dimpy Aunty.

'Absolutely, that I completely do, and the coolest thing about my work is that when I talk to people, whether in college or corporate offices, the organization has to sign the contract that no superior authority can be present. So for many, it's like spitting out what they have kept inside of them for years,' Agastya smiles.

'That's true. This type of atmosphere improves the effectiveness of the session, as what is baggage for the employees is outside the room, unaware of the discussions happening within the four walls,' says Dimpy Aunty. Arjun looks at her, thinking she has said the most sensible thing in the recent times.

They enjoy the food with the humour that Dimpy Aunty, as usual, brings to the table. Agastya spends a delightful time with all of them before he flies for work to Bengaluru in the evening, even though he is still worried about Addya. He wants her to get the work contract in Mumbai so that he can talk to the lawyer to get her case shifted there.

Nineteen

Love is not just about giving surprising or making unexpected gestures for your loved ones. It is also the accumulation of the tiny little things you do for someone that counts. Love is not about intensity, it is about consistency and how long you can maintain that. Agastya has planned to catch a direct flight from Bengaluru to Guwahati after his work to meet Tarjani. They have mutually decided to spend some quality time together there. Tarjani has been significantly preoccupied with the installation of the new artwork in Guwahati.

Back at work, Agastya delivers his speech to the people sitting in the compact auditorium. He checks his wristwatch for the fifth time. He needs to catch the flight to meet Tarjani. He is anxious.

He continues to the audience, '…and humans are curious creatures. We all focus so much on the future while failing to live in the present. If you are nodding your head left to right, be honest with yourself. Has there been a moment in your life when you thought, "I can't wait to get out of school and get a job so that I can take care of myself and do what I love"? You always had this thought; we all did. Moreover, our parents inculcated this in us right from our childhood.

'Then, when you finally bag your dream job, it becomes

a monotonous routine, much to your disappointment. You convince yourself that you are working for a better future by missing out on what life has to offer to you in the present. Many such projects come and go, but you are left with no memories to cherish. And then, you convince yourself that you'll have a life after your kids grow up and get settled. You will have a life after you retire. You need to wake up now and save yourself from falling into this trap. Do not let your whole life be about "I'll be happy when…". Be happy now.

'Dreaming for a brighter future is an inescapable quest, but not at the cost of sacrificing the tiny pleasures you derive from the present. No level of preparation for the future can ready you for the surprises and curveballs that life will throw at you. The more prepared you are, the more you will try to mould life into a normal, expected experience. Take care of the fundamentals—for the rest, let life take you on an exhilarating ride!'

The audience in the auditorium applauds thunderously at the conclusion of the speech.

Agastya switches on his cellphone as he walks out of the auditorium and connects to the recent number on the call log. He impatiently waits for Tarjani to receive his call. He knows that in the last couple of days, rather weeks, they have not been in touch—this is increasingly bothering him. Time is running out of his hand before he can even realize it.

This is human nature—people we care about most make us miss them the most as well. Folding his blazer between his ribs and hand, carelessly, he hurriedly walks to hail a cab to the airport. Now he understands how Tarjani must have felt when she would call him, and he wouldn't attend her calls. He becomes impatient and dials the number for the umpteenth time. The call goes unanswered. Agastya stops trying and catches a cab to the airport.

♥

Pushing the blazer back in the trolley bag, Agastya looks ahead at the queue of people standing to collect their boarding pass. The queue seems endless. He glances at the giant display clock. It is quarter to five. He cradles the phone between his ear and shoulder, calling Tarjani again, and drags the trolley bag.

Tarjani answers the phone this time. With a deep voice, she says, 'Hi.'

'Why were you not taking my calls? I have been calling you for an hour,' Agastya asks her in a vexed tone.

'I was in a meeting,' she says casually and continues. 'So you finally found some time for me? By the way, the event was pretty good. Many people appreciated my work. They also enquired about who represented my work earlier. I wanted to tell them that the person does not care anymore.'

'It just slipped out of my mind. I was continuously travelling for work,' says Agastya regretfully. Had he been a little more cautious, he would have noted it down in his calendar. Had he been in Tarjani's place, he would probably react outrageously too. He had plans to be with her but had booked the ticket for the evening thinking that the event was tomorrow.

'Oh, you forgot. Your behaviour over the last couple of

weeks has changed,' Tarjani is a little unsettled because she was expecting him to be with her.

It was not just the beauty of her work that had helped her seize the deal. Agastya's contribution at the last moment to represent her work with his eccentric skills had also made a huge difference. Otherwise, bringing it to prominence would have been a difficult task. Therefore, not just Tarjani but everyone wanted to congratulate Agastya when Tarjani told them the real story behind it. She had missed him terribly.

'I just forgot because I had some work to finish,' Agastya is disappointed with himself. His self-judgement baffles him more. At the same time, he starts thinking about what the lawyer had said to him in the morning about transferring Addya's case to Mumbai. He feels a tight band around his forehead.

'You forgot. I expected it anyway. I wouldn't be surprised if you forget me also someday.' Her cynicism speaks volumes. It hurts Agastya but he does not react much because he does not want to unnecessarily fight over it.

'I am grieved by my act, and I also realize that I am behaving differently,' Agastya admits.

'That's okay. But we have known each other for a long time now, we know almost everything about each other's life. What is bothering you? I tell you everything, but it seems like you do not do the same.'

'There is nothing to talk about. Why are you stretching it unnecessarily?' Agastya gets impatient.

'Agastya, I am not stretching anything unnecessarily. You are trying to fix everything and not discussing with me. If you have problems in your life, you should talk about it. Would you not expect me to do the same?' Tarjani asks a question that no man can answer in this situation.

'Tarjani we are different people. We have different personalities. You like to express, and I don't,' he says. He knows his words will hurt her.

'There's absolutely no point arguing with you. You always end up saying this,' says Tarjani.

'Because there is no problem. Had you been in my situation, you would probably understand it better. Nevertheless, forget it now.' The lady in front of him in the queue turns around and looks at Agastya.

'You have all your space, but that doesn't mean you own that space completely. Am I not a part of it?' Tarjani questons.

The conversation seems to be going nowhere. Tarjani wants to know if something is bothering him since the past few weeks.

'Yes, you are a part of it. Otherwise, I would have never waited for someone for three hours just to say hi,' Agastya slowly starts losing his temper.

'Sweets! That's what I am saying. You can't fix everything alone,' Tarjani says while she packs her bag and gets ready to leave from Guwahati to Mumbai.

'Listen! I got a call from the lawyer, and he is unsure about filing an appeal to transfer Addya's case,' says Agastya.

'Why? He had mentioned that this was possible, isn't it?' Tarjani questions worriedly. She pauses. Her words now depict acute concern for the situation.

'Yes, but he asked for some valid documents that show that Addya has reasons to live in Mumbai. And one reason I could think of was work here, but everything is taking too much time. This is just not working out…'

'Can't she be a part of Uzaro? She can be, right? I am

in the process of getting things ready for approval. It will only take a few more days according to the officials. So I just need to extend some formalities for Addya,' Tarjani offers.

'Is it possible?' Agastya enquires.

'It is, and you could have discussed this with me before. I might not be the solution to your problem, but I can try my best to be a helping hand,' Tarjani exclaims.

'You are already doing it.' His worry turns into calmness. He asks, 'When are you coming to Mumbai? I am excited to see you.'

'Just taking my flight in a couple of hours or so,' says Tarjani, leaving the hotel room.

'Then I'll see you in Mumbai. Why don't you come home? Addya is also there. She will feel good to see you.'

Agastya comes out of the queue, dragging the trolley, and sits on the bench. He was supposed to fly to Guwahati a moment ago, but now checks for the corporate claims he has made that month. He looks at the gate and makes a decision. Almost everyone has left to board the flight for Guwahati. There is an announcement—'This is the final boarding call for Mr Agastya travelling with flight AI37 to Guwahati. Please proceed to gate number 3 immediately. Thank you.'

Agastya ignores the announcement completely, and turns around and approaches the counter to get a ticket for Mumbai on priority.

Twenty

Agastya and Tarjani arrive at Arjun's apartment after 10:00 p.m. They follow Arjun to the hall where Addya is having dinner with Ved. She has a new companion who makes her laugh all day long.

Arjun, Ved and Addya are overwhelmed to see them. Agastya and Ved share a quick hug and he drags his bag to the corner. Tarjani follows.

'Hey, how are you?' Tarjani greets Addya. A warm embrace is all they need to reminisce whatever little time they had spent together. It seems like they have met after ages.

'I am good. How you are doing? Take your time,' Tarjani says, smiling at the way Addya is gorging on food.

'No, I am almost done,' she replies, still chewing. She wipes her hands.

'So good to see you,' Addya says.

'Good to see you too. So, how's Mumbai treating the new girl in the city?' Tarjani feels good to see optimism on Addya's face and in her voice. Mumbai suits her.

'Nothing special, just eating and resting all day. That is the mantra for now. Thanks to Arjun. He has been spoiling me day and night. He has definitely become a better chef, thanks to my appetite.' They both laugh, looking at Arjun.

'Thank you,' Arjun addresses Addya dramatically, 'always at your service,' and then, he grins at Tarjani, saying, 'and now at yours too.'

Arjun asks Agastya and Tarjani to freshen up before he can serve them dinner.

Tarjani splashes some cold water on her face and immediately feels better. It was a tiresome yet productive day. The food is served on the table while Addya is on a call with her mother. Meanwhile, Tarjani is thinking about expediting the documentation work for expansion in Mumbai. She remembers the conversation she had with her mother about coming home. Her mother had also enquired about Agastya and had invited him to Lucknow.

She assumed that Agastya would not have any problem meeting her family. Perhaps it was against his family's values but considering the turmoil Addya had to go through simply because she abided by the family's traditions, she knows Agastya wouldn't care about it. Traditions are considered valuable only when they ensure welfare of the individual and the community as a whole, otherwise they suffocate. Rituals and traditions need to adapt to the changing times, just like our appearances and outlook.

'What happened?' Agastya asks, with concern writ on his face. He wishes to share something with Tarjani but he pauses when he sees a frown on her face.

A lawsuit has been filed against Agastya for attempting to cause harm to Bali. Things seem to be getting out of hand. He has not informed anyone yet.

'Nothing, I have been travelling quite a lot lately. A little discomfort is expected. I am fine,' Tarjani attempts to comfort him with a smile. She pats her face dry and gulps down a glass of water.

'So what's next? Are you going to rent out some place here in Mumbai for the gallery?' Agastya tries to find out more about the expansion she is planning.

'Still thinking,' replies Tarjani.

'We can discuss with Arjun as he knows a lot about Mumbai.'

'Yeah.'

'I am sorry about what I said in the afternoon,' Agastya says, feeling apologetic. He had just been pissed off then. Tarjani pauses; she wants to say something but ends up saying, 'That's okay.'

In a relationship, when you start considering your words before speaking, and when words don't seem enough to describe emotions, that is the time to nurture it. They enjoy a late-night dinner and then all of them head to meet Dimpy Aunty as she has especially invited Tarjani for dessert.

On a rainy summer night, while Arjun, Ved and Agastya are sleeping in the hall, Addya in one room and Tarjani in the other, Agastya gets up and goes to her room. After a few knocks, Tarjani opens the door. The wind is blowing and it is raining heavily. The room is filled with the smell of damp earth.

'What happened?'

'Nothing. I just wanted to spend some time with you.'

'Come inside,' Tarjani locks the door and switches on the lamp next to the bed. Agastya sits on the bed.

'Are you not sleepy? It's the middle of the night,' he asks.

'Not really, and I'm pretty sure you are not sleepy either,' she squints.

'So, is there something you want to tell me? I can sense it,' he asks.

'Umm yeah. So, firstly, do not get me wrong, but a few friends of mine already know you well. I am going home next week, Agastya. I need to tell my mom and brother about you,' Tarjani says. She is pretty optimistic about her relationship with him. However, she needs assurance from him. Words are more powerful than emotions because they initiate assurances. Tarjani does not wish to unnecessarily complicate this conversation and continues after a pause, 'I am not forcing you to do anything. I know you have other priorities, and so do I. But we can at least talk to our families about it. Once families are involved and agree, we both can take our own time.'

'I agree with you, but this isn't the right time considering the miserable plight that I am stuck in,' says Agastya.

'That does not matter to me. You will always be the same for me. Otherwise, I would not have spent nights with you, sharing the same bed. I am sure you love me too,' she says confidently.

'Of course, I do. But there's something you need to know before you finalize anything. I have a case pending against me...'

'What?' Why?' she exclaims.

'Apparently, because I threatened Bali, but there is nothing to worry about. The lawyer is sorting it out, and I have been called to be present in the police station to answer some questions. I am just worried about Addya. But I do understand your position.'

Not many of us have close relationships in a world full of unstable feelings based on swiping right and left. Infidelity is widespread in relationships these days, and Tarjani doesn't care about anything except for the fact that they love each other.

'I'm always there with you,' Tarjani embraces him.

'Always love, more than yesterday,' he says as he kisses her. Agastya does not want to let go of anything and regret later. They will figure it out together—how to stay close to each other, how to keep each other happy. Agastya does not wish to leave any stone unturned, forgetting everything that he has experienced in the past. They both know—together they are fire; apart, they are nothing.

'I want to marry you, will you?' he asks in between kisses.

'That's what I dream about,' she kisses him back. They both lie down while she rests her head on his chest. Agastya is staring at the ceiling, listening to her talk about their future. Tarjani also mentions that the next morning she will ask Addya if she would like to work for Uzaro and manage the Mumbai operations.

Agastya asks, 'Can you make Addya a partner in Uzaro, Mumbai?'

Tarjani is silent for a few seconds and replies, 'Well, she doesn't know anything about it yet—procurement or how to manage any function individually.'

Agastya replies, 'She is a quick learner, I'm sure she will manage.'

Tarjani states, 'I started Uzaro because of Aarav...'

Before Tarjani can say anything more, Agastya interrupts her, 'Okay, no worries, it was just a thought. You know better. And anyway, I am thankful to you. I will now step out. You should also rest.'

They both hug each other, and Agastya steps out.

Next morning, when Addya hands a cup of tea to her, Tarjani says, 'I have an offer for you. I am setting up the Mumbai office for Uzaro very soon and was thinking if you could be a part of it. I would like to offer you a partnership. I hope you will not reject it.' She smiles.

'What? I have no idea about any of this. I mean, creativity and I are poles apart,' says Addya, very unsure about the offer.

'That's how we learn. We'll do it,' Tarjani assures her.

Twenty-one

Agastya discusses the plans Tarjani had shared with him before he leaves for work. Her wish is to expand her connections in this city, which can indeed bring her more work and recognition. Agastya had hoped that this would happen to Tarjani as she was ambitious. Addya, too, would do well. Trust comes with love in a relationship. Though Tarjani is still unsure about the exact location of her new Mumbai office, she is happy to have a new companion in this venture. Addya always wished to stand on her own feet and it is not difficult to convince her to join hands with Tarjani. This only encourages her to chase those buried aspirations.

'Please take care of yourself,' Agastya says to Addya, while saying goodbye to little Takshika.

'I am coming to drop you,' Addya gets ready to drop Agastya to the airport while he waits for his cab to arrive.

'I'll go. Do not worry. You take care of the little one,' he says.

'It's a matter of an hour. Arjun will take care of her,' Addya says. Arjun nods.

'Babysitter, good job.' Agastya looks at Arjun and continues, 'What are your plans after that?'

'Tarjani and I will see Addya at the seaside in an hour.'

Agastya's phone beeps and they walk towards the cab.

'By the way, what obsession do women have with the sea and the waves?' Agastya laughs. The cab driver accelerates; they can see him smile in the front mirror.

'No obsession, just that we girls have some crazy plans,' Addya blinks at him. He is pleased to witness an optimistic change in her.

'Good to know,' says Agastya.

Addya drops him and then heads to South Mumbai to spend some time with herself before Arjun and Tarjani join her.

Addya walks on the esplanade along the road at the Marine Drive and then stands by the sea. The air is fresh and the view after sunset is radiant. Everyone seems to head to Marine Drive to get some fresh air as dusk envelops the city. She turns her gaze to the mesmerizing view of the skyline defined against the sea. It is more beautiful than the description Addya's friends would give in the canteen during her college days. They all dreamt of trying their luck in Bollywood.

We all desire to become a hero or heroine once in our lifetime, isn't it? Destiny has made her one in her own life. We are all destined to die the moment we are born; it is what we do in between that really counts. She reflects all that life has thrown at her in that long walk she takes along the sea. Addya truly needs this time to reduce the background music playing in her head, and simply listen to her heart.

The world is full of empty people who are busy in their own lives. A weak person is terrified to see hurdles on the way, while a winner perceives hurdles to be milestones as he sets to accomplish them one after the other. She wishes to be away from the dark and daunting thoughts of her past. However, there is a spark of light glowing within her, waiting for the right moment to shine brightly. Addya tries to make herself believe in her incumbent potential. A message flashes on her cellphone. It is Arjun.

> I have taken the baby bag that has extra diapers, wipes, milk powder, hot water and sanitizer. Is there anything else I need to carry?

Addya smiles while replying.

> Perfect :)
> Man knows everything.

A new message flashes instantly.

> Also, listen! Can you come down to Bandra?
> Tarjani and I can see you there. Dimpy Aunty is also joining us.

> Works!
> See you.

With the irate sea on one side and the dazzling streets of Bandra on the other, Dimpy Aunty spends most of her Sundays here with her daughters, Anushka and Angira. However, today they both have taken the bold decision of not coming, so the victim is the one she usually finds during emergency—Arjun.

They are enjoying a walk on the beach and taking in the sea breeze. Perhaps, later she will help Arjun shop in Bandra for his upcoming events. He takes a few steps holding the baby who is sleeping in a carrier while Dimpy Aunty enthusiastically fills her shopping bags with street items.

Arjun says, 'By the way, are you sure Tarjani can mention your home address as her office address, as the Mumbai office is not yet decided and she needs to have a reference address for further paperwork?'

Arjun wants to know her opinion. He does not want her to be stuck in a formality.

'That's your home too, Arjun. It's the wisest decision to take at the moment,' Dimpy Aunty does not think before answering. She pauses before adding, 'You know, I ran a boutique long ago from the same household.'

Arjun simply bows down to her and remarks, 'Is there anything you haven't done in your lifetime?'

She chuckles. 'Ask Tarjani what plans she's got. By the way, she was supposed to join us, where is she?' she asks.

'She had to meet someone. She will be here soon.'

'Also, Agastya was telling me over messages that Tarjani is involving Addya with her. I am glad. The change will do her good,' says Dimpy Aunty.

Dimpy Aunty calls Addya.

'Hello Aunty,' Addya says.

'How much time will it take you to come to Bandra?' asks Dimpy Aunty on the phone call.

'Maybe thirty minutes,' she responds using her analytical

skills without knowing the exact distance. In a few days, she has discovered that in Mumbai, distance is measured by time and not by the actual distance.

'Are you nearby?' Dimpy Aunty asks her.

'Not sure, but I am just roaming around Marine Drive.'

'Next time, you can call me if you don't want to spend time alone. Don't be alone. Well, I am here in Bandra with Arjun and waiting for Tarjani and you to join us. Let me show you today how rich people buy the cheapest clothes by street shopping,' she laughs.

'That's great. Surely. I will take a cab and see you there?' Addya takes her handbag and gets up, looking for a cab.

'Come quickly,' Dimpy Aunty teases her.

'Can't wait. See you soon,' says Addya and dials Tarjani's number immediately after the call.

♥

Arjun finds a beachside café that he loves and asks Dimpy Aunty to relax over a cup of cappuccino.

'Sometimes it's just so soothing to sit and do nothing. Can you feel it?' says Dimpy Aunty, pushing the cup aside and stretching her legs on the sofa.

'If you are talking about this moment, I don't think that we have done nothing,' pointing towards the bags lying beside the table, Arjun says sarcastically.

'Hm...hm,' she nods.

'I think I deserve more than just a nod, don't I? I skipped my cricket match in the evening. I may lose my place in the team.'

'As if you were going to make a century.'

They both laugh. Dimpy Aunty enjoys her coffee while they wait for Addya and Tarjani to join them.

♥

Addya steps in, extending her hands to hug Dimpy Aunty. Arjun waves at her.

Dimpy Aunty welcomes her with a kiss on the cheek.

'I am so happy to see you,' Addya says to Dimpy Aunty and blinks at Arjun.

'Yes, it's been long since we saw each other; what are you doing these days?' Dimpy Aunty asks her to sit next to Arjun.

'Thank you so much for taking care of her,' Addya approaches Takshika.

'Wait! Let me unhook the carrier,' says Arjun.

Dimpy Aunty burps, making them laugh. Arjun looks at her and sees her smile. In the age of unhooking something else, he is unhooking a baby carrier.

'So where is Tarjani?' Addya asks.

'She was supposed to join us but she got stuck with some work and then in traffic, so she will be late,' explains Arjun.

'No problem, I anyway wanted to talk to you alone,' says Dimpy Aunty and continues, 'so how's Mumbai treating you?'

'We have just been roaming around since the day I landed here,' she looks at Arjun.

'Yeah,' he says.

'Great, enjoy yourself and take care of your health.'

'Yeah, trying to...'

Arjun stands up to get a second round of coffee for them and a sandwich for Addya while Dimpy Aunty confronts Addya about the previous night.

'Why were you crying yesterday night?' Dimpy Aunty asks her.

'Arjun told you?'

'Don't tell him. He got emotional when we were talking about you. He looks tough but I have known him for years. He is very sensitive.'

'Nothing, I was just worried about my future and the future of my baby,' Addya looks at Takshika who is in her arms.

'This is my second marriage. I got married at a very early age and things worsened just like yours. Then I realized that a woman without a man is crippled in this fucking society. Ironically, the same society celebrates the glory and grit of Goddess Durga,' Dimpy Aunty highlights the harsh reality.

Addya nods.

She continues, 'You know, we all suffer from a disease that doesn't kill us but eats us everyday, like a termite, that too, without our conscious knowledge. It is called regret. So, never regret things irrespective of how big or small they are. For three years, I tried not to remember too much because there was a lot to remember, and I did not want to fall behind with the events of my life. I still do not have what I expected in life. But I do not have regrets,' finishes Dimpy Aunty.

'Everyone always said that I would make my parents proud when I grew up. So, the name "Addya" was given to me by my father. How soon I was judged when things didn't turn out as I had planned!' she says in pain. Arjun joins them without any interruption and listens to their conversation intently.

Dimpy Aunty holds her hands and says, 'Always remember one thing, self-love is a prerequisite to loving others. Self-love is important because when it is four in the morning and you are crying alone in your bed, who is going to be with you? You. You have to pull yourself together and find the strength to walk again. And at the end of the day, you are all you have. No one has a better idea about your capabilities and strengths. Perhaps the toughest thing to do in life is to affirm how remarkable you really can be, believe in yourself, and then to incorporate this awareness into your attitude and personality. Store your pain and let it come out for the right reasons.'

Addya agrees with every word she hears from Dimpy Aunty, but she cannot make herself believe her own words. It is human nature to doubt ourselves in difficult situations. But we also have to trust ourselves to get out of those situations.

'Thank you,' she squeezes Dimpy Aunty's hand. The hold is that of affection, of conviction. Today, she has developed a stronger bond with Dimpy Aunty. Arjun is stunned listening to her. He does not know how he should react—if he should feel bad about what happened to her or happy that she is with him, safe and alive, and she is still full of life, full of positivity.

Addya says, 'I agree with your words but it has been a difficult task for me to take decisions. I am always worried if I am making the right ones.'

Dimpy Aunty continues, 'So, do what you feel like. Do not expect that anyone will come to help you. I may sound harsh but I am bluntly speaking the truth that I have encountered and experienced. So take your time, make your decision, and never look back after that. And do not give a fuck about anyone—that's the subtle art of living a good life. Mark Manson said this in 2016 in his book but I have been practising it for years. You know, we never lose by working hard on things, we only lose when we stop and start looking back and weeping about things that happened in the past. And do not get distracted by wishes and expectations, they will never be fulfilled. You can trust me on this.

'I still do not have a vegetable garden. I still have not been on a world tour. It is completely fine if you are not getting what you dreamt of. A hero is not a hero because he always wins, a hero is a hero because he keeps trying even in the worst situations. Well, in our case it is a heroine.' She winks.

Addya smiles and nods. 'How beautifully you simplify things. I should have met you before.'

Dimpy Aunty's words reflect the truth and reveal her soul—loving and positive, which is very rare. She speaks what she thinks.

'Arjun is lucky to have you around. I have heard only funny things about you. This is something Arjun never told me,' Addya feels strong after listening to Dimpy Aunty.

'He is my knight in shining armour and I have seen him make some blunders as well. I am definitely going to tell you some day,' says Dimpy Aunty, smiling.

'I would love to hear. You know, sometimes I think I should have considered the proposals in my college days.'

'Yes, you could have because times have changed and love marriages are more successful than arranged ones these days. This is because when you go for love marriage you already know that you are ready to compromise on things because you are responsible for your choice, not someone else. In case of arranged marriages, you give up on things easily and put the blame either on the family or your partner. You become weak about your choices; that is completely natural. All your life you hear people say, "Choose the profession you enjoy, not just because someone has told you to do". Then, why does the same family fail to understand this simple logic about marriage?'

♥

'Hello-ooo,' Tarjani shouts from the entrance of the café.

'Hello, how are you, Miss Entrepreneur?' Dimpy Aunty waves at her without moving from her place.

'I am good. Hope you guys are doing well too,' she embraces her tightly and sits next to her.

'I have heard you are doing amazing work. Congratulations,' Dimpy Aunty feels proud.

'All because of your blessings. I am doing well but too many things are happening, so just trying to manage. I am sure you know it. Now I have her, so we will be on the rollercoaster ride together,' Tarjani says in excitement.

'Thank you. Thank you,' Addya responds.

'I am so happy for you guys,' with a cheerful voice and a proud expression, Dimpy Aunty wishes them good luck.

'Agastya told me that you are facing certain issues with the registration of your new office in Mumbai,' adds Dimpy Aunty.

'I just need to get it registered with an address and once I get some more clients, I'll get a permanent office and transfer the address. I have asked a few of my old clients, let's see if any of them agree,' Tarjani tells her the plan. She is prudent and has foresight. She has things in place. She is not just hard-working, but smart when it comes to executing ideas as well.

'You can use my home address,' says Dimpy Aunty.

Tarjani looks at Arjun and then at Dimpy Aunty.

Surprised, she says, 'Really?' Her expression changes to a wide smile.

'That's why I said it,' Dimpy Aunty grins.

'I had heard this from Arjun before, but you truly are the solution to everything,' Tarjani accepts her offer with gratitude. She gets up and wraps her up in a hug.

'I completely agree with that,' Addya grins.

'That's not always true,' says Arjun and remembers when she had illicitly printed his books to get more readers. He just wants to forget that nightmare. They both laugh.

'But most of the times...,' responds Dimpy Aunty.

'All the best. You must be hungry, let's celebrate with a brownie?' announces Dimpy Aunty.

'Why not?' says Tarjani. Arjun gets up to order while Dimpy Aunty continues her discussion with Addya and Tarjani. They all have a good time.

Siblings play an enormous role in cementing a relationship. Together, Arjun and Agastya lay the first brick of the foundation for Addya to build her future once again.

Twenty-two

Addya is feeling slightly nostalgic before beginning her new journey with Tarjani. A gold medalist in her college days, she had built her career as a marketing consultant and then as a professor, and is now extending her interest in artworks. This can be complicated for anyone. However, she is not worried about the fact that she never thought of herself as an artistic person. The idea is not to come up with a masterpiece. She does not have to show her work to anyone. Just expressing herself and creating something original out of her feelings or mood is enough. Some therapists use artistic expression to facilitate therapy. She is going to counsel herself with the help of this medium—creative art therapy. This partnership with Tarjani will also help her in legal formalities so that she can get a fair trial.

♥

Tarjani and Addya are spending their day at Arjun's apartment. The hall is messy and it is going to remain in that state for another couple of weeks, until Tarjani manages to lay her hands on a few more prominent clients, like the one she cracked recently. A set of watercolours, acrylic paints, an art pad, and some brushes are lying on the floor. Addya picks up the art pad and some colour pencils.

'It's okay. You are not going to do this,' says Tarjani, sitting next to her on the floor. She used to teach her brother, Aarav, the same way in their childhood days.

'Yeah, but it feels really good to hold it. It already makes me feel like an artist,' Addya smiles as she picks up colourful clay and gently kneads it to eliminate the air bubbles. She rolls it into a ball, keeping her fingers and thumbs moist. She laughs.

'You seem to be on track,' Tarjani appreciates the movements of her wrist.

'I used to play with clay as a child but didn't know then that someday it would become my profession. I didn't even know that someone could make money out of this,' Addya laughs. She seems to be enjoying herself.

Tarjani gives her an old picture of an abstract that she had obtained from the garbage collector. She tears the old picture into tiny pieces and assembles them in a creative pattern. She instructs Addya to fill the empty space with colourful clay.

'Broken things have more value in this world,' Arjun says, passing by.

'Agreed. Who knows that better than you?' Tarjani smiles and adds, 'Though not because it is broken, but because these artworks are a sign of hope that broken things can be fixed or modified beautifully, isn't it?'

Arjun smiles at Tarjani. Addya feels stronger and Tarjani, lighter. This collaboration is not just with Addya, it is with Arjun, Dimpy Aunty and Anushka.

♥

'I know Agastya is a good man, the one who has read books on pregnancy and enjoyed late-night food craving runs, and who has bundled up when I was having a heat flash and wanted to crank the air conditioning all the way up in the middle of December. And let's not forget, he made sure the pickles were safe!' Addya tells her how Agastya helped her in her worst days.

'Really? I know he is very loving and kind but we have not been able to spend much time together,' Tarjani says and she wants Addya to talk more about him. Agastya has just not been a sibling to her, he has even mothered her, playing dual roles many times even when she had an amazing mother to support her unconditionally.

A woman needs a man who remains the same even when the situation changes. There are innumerable times when you go through a hard time and you need at least one person in your life to encourage you and to be a sponge that can absorb all the negativity. Agastya is that one person for her.

'So, when is your family coming to meet us? Or else, we all can come to meet aunty and Aarav,' Addya asks her and wants to take the lead for Agastya. She knows how much Agastya loves her.

'Whenever it is convenient for you,' Tarjani smiles and tries hard to hide the fact that she is blushing. It is a dream for every girl to marry the one she loves, the rest is just a compromise people settle for these days.

'Great,' Addya begins to plan in her head.

'Well, for now, we have to wrap this up,' Tarjani says and prioritizes what is more important at the moment. 'Are you coming with me tomorrow to Kala Ghoda?'

'What did you say?' Addya almost laughs. 'What is that?'

Addya has heard this name for the first time.

Tarjani chuckles, 'It is a prominent art festival. Many things for us to see and learn there. Come with me if you are free? I am also new to it but it will be a good experience for us.'

'I would love to. I have else nothing to do. But can I also take Takshika along?'

'Of course.'

'Cool. Let's go tomorrow.'

They work till late at night and then they decide to call it a day.

'It is two in the night, we should sleep,' Tarjani says, looking at Addya.

'Yeah, we have to get up early tomorrow,' she approaches the kitchen to get water.

'Yeah. Yeah.'

Addya takes some medicine and enters her room. The door closes.

♥

Addya's mind is in a turmoil but she knows that she will feel better if she vents. She will find an escape if she gets her creative juices flowing through art, writing, music, or a favourite hobby. It will probably also help her get rid of the sleeping pills. Addya is unable to sleep; she continues to toss and turn on the bed, thinking about her life. She has almost spent the whole night working on the artwork with Tarjani. She remembers her college days when she used to do everything, from getting sponsors to preparing the stage for the fest. That time, she used to do it for others. Now, she is doing it for herself. It is all about perspective. Isn't it?

Kala Ghoda is a nine-day long event held in South Mumbai. It is all about emotions on canvases, Indian handicrafts, memoirs and trinkets, all colourfully scattered. It is a festival that celebrates the emergence of artists. Addya is spellbound by the art on display. She and Tarjani wish to bring some good news home today if they get a chance to display their work. Even Dimpy Aunty has strongly recommended this place.

Every piece of artwork carries a unique message. Tarjani especially likes a piece of art that subtly displays the ill effects of colours. Some of the artworks, while beautiful, give her goosebumps. From children to adults, there is something for everyone. However, there are also young students who instead of appreciating art, climb on it for the mere purpose of a selfie. Addya walks ahead to enquire about the space she can get and display the artwork Tarjani was suggesting her to begin.

Tarjani tells her to lead. 'Your way…I'll hold her,' she says and takes Takshika in her arms.

Addya is a little nervous, and scrutinizing around, she approaches one of the counters, which seems like a temporary office for commercial purposes. There are hoardings, amongst other things on the floor, waiting to be installed.

'Hi, who is the organizer?' she asks.

A man turns around and looks at her. 'Yes, ma'am, please

tell me?' he asks her thoughtfully.

'I want to enquire about something...,' biting her lower lip, she pauses and continues, 'I am from Uzaro. We create artwork and they are well recognized by people. We have worked on some prominent projects; we recently did something special for the Taj hotels. Our uniqueness is that we create artwork from broken things, and no two artworks are the same. So, I want to display them here. Can you help me with the process?' she asks curiously.

Tarjani is standing far away, observing the conversation Addya is having with the man. She knows that this is the only way Addya will learn. There were rejections when Tarjani started but rejections just prepare you for success.

'It's a long process, you have to register and pay the fee, which is minimum fifty thousand plus taxes depending on how much space you want. I would suggest you register for the next event because all the registrations are closed. But I can suggest something,' his voice lowers, and he says, 'if you see any counter here which belongs to the same category, you can collaborate.'

The spark in her eyes seems to fizzle.

'Thank you,' Addya smiles and tries to convince a few people who do not seem to believe in collaborating with them. This is her first attempt at such a venture, and she has mixed feelings. But she does not give up, and turns around to look for Tarjani.

Suddenly, Addya notices Tarjani incessantly messaging someone. Tarjani says she wishes to go home and that she is not feeling well. Addya takes Takshika back in her arms. The expression on her face troubles Addya. They immediately head back home.

♥

With knitted brows and moist eyes, Tarjani shouts on a phone call, checking at the same time if Addya or Arjun can hear her.

'Why did you doubt me? You don't trust me, right?' Her words are harsh, and her face is red with anger. There are beads of sweat on her forehead. Agastya does not understand what has happened and what she is talking about. Even in the most stressful situation, Tarjani never yells.

'What happened Tarjani?' Agastya asks and tries to remember what he has done that Tarjani will not appreciate. He is at his wit's end. A shiver runs down his spine when he hears her fierce voice. He remains silent.

'You could have checked with me directly if you needed to know if Addya's name is on the official paper or not. That is what you wanted, and I agreed to it. And now you are enquiring from others rather than asking me. What is that?'

The series of questions makes Agastya numb and now he regrets calling Uzaro in Lucknow to get the information—he did not even get it.

'I didn't doubt…' says Agastya.

'Agastya! Uzaro was a dedication to my brother who is on a wheelchair right now. Aarav might not even appreciate the things I have done for you, but I did them because you wanted that. I respect her, and I would have been more than happy to help but I never wanted to be a medium,' Tarjani says. She feels like running away from this place.

'I didn't lie to you. I had just called…,' Agastya responds. He wants her to understand his situation.

'Yes, you called my office to check. It is not about enquiring, it's about the trust between us, or whether we even have any. I loved you more than anyone else in my life. You always said that work comes first but I didn't even care because you were always my priority.'

'I was about to tell you Tarjani… You are misunderstanding me,' Agastya says. Standing in the corner of the hotel room, he regrets what he has done. His intentions were never wrong, but his way was.

'We are in a relationship and you always wanted me to meet your family, but you never cared to meet my mother even when she specially invited you. Now, I do not even know if you are sure about me. If it is not working out, we must stop. I will still help Addya. Being with me is not necessary for that to happen. I just hate you…,' tears roll down her cheeks as she continues, 'I do not know if I should cry or laugh at myself. When you came into my life, I had almost forgotten the issues that I had in my life, but now it all feels like a joke.'

It is 11:45 p.m. and an awake Addya has heard everything. Listening to her conversation with Agastya, she goes into her room, blaming herself and her situations in life. She wants to talk to Tarjani but she also does not want to make her uncomfortable.

Tarjani disconnects the call. Agastya messages Tarjani on all platforms, hoping she responds somewhere. He holds the hand rest of the sofa tightly and sits. He bursts into tears. His lips quiver as he feels numbness engulf his body. He does not know what to do now or how to react to this. He knows he has behaved selfishly in order to resolve things; he understands now that everything he does is not always smart.

Agastya wants to call Addya and tell her about this, but he pauses thinking what he will talk about. There is no one in the room to listen to his feelings. He holds both his hands up as if praying and bangs his own head on the side of the sofa. Agastya immediately calls Arjun, seeking his help.

The person who is the closest becomes the strangest when feelings turn upside down. Considering it to be her fault that Agastya and Tarjani were in this mess, Addya gathers her courage and knocks on the door of Tarjani's room in the morning with numerous thoughts running in her mind.

'Hi,' says Tarjani.

'Good morning. The early bird is late today?' says Addya, looking at the bed which seemed like nobody slept on it.

'Nothing. Just feeling sluggish. So, stretched my day,' she responds, checking her cellphone.

'Are you sure? Because you had to go for some visits, right? Or is there anything you want to discuss?' Addya takes a few steps and waits for her to look at her.

'Nothing, nothing. I am good. I am actually heading out to meet a few friends. Need to wrap up a few things before I take my flight to Lucknow day after tomorrow,' Tarjani is feeling suffocated since yesterday. She still avoids eye contact because if her eyes meet Addya's, truth will inevitably spill out. Addya decides to start the conversation.

'Listen Tarjani! It's not that I need anything from you. Of course, we have a great bond. I need your help only if you want to provide it. However, I do understand that I have been a barrier between you and Agastya.'

Tarjani listens to Addya intently.

Addya holds both her hands in an apology. It is an uncomfortable moment for Tarjani. They both are feeling vulnerable.

'Don't ever do that. You are older to me, and yes, we share a bond. I felt terrible because Agastya didn't confide in me completely,' Tarjani says gently.

'There are a few things we do without thinking about their consequences. This is one of those things Agastya has done for me. He is an inspiration for all the brothers who love their sisters but cannot express. But sometimes he starts overthinking. I do not know if I should blame him or the situation for that but at the same time, it's also true that he adores you. He randomly takes your name in a conversation and starts talking about you. He loves you the most,' Addya shares those instances when Agastya has talked about Tarjani to the family.

♥

There is one thing special about being in a healthy relationship with someone—no matter how much pain is coursing through your veins, you always help the other person forget his or her pain. And at the end of the day when that happens, your pain also goes away. That is the beauty of a relationship when it has developed over a period of time.

'Now get up and call Agastya. Otherwise he will leave all his work and come again to see you,' Addya says, trying to lighten her mood.

'Yeah, actually,' she laughs.

'And it is Sunday so Arjun is taking us out for breakfast, get ready. Anushka is also joining us.'

'Is Dimpy Aunty also coming?' asks Tarjani.

Arjun joins the conversation as he passes by, 'It seems you guys are already best friends. She is not coming because she is busy today.'

'She has good vibes.'

'That she does.'

Addya leaves the room, and so do all the doubts and worries. One good thing about taking time with a relationship and turning it into a strong one is that even in crisis, when things go awry, that person always stands up for you. It is rare but it is possible when two people work on a relationship.

Twenty-three

The best conversations take place around a table and we always have many things to discuss with our loved ones. Arjun believes that sitting around a table and breaking bread together has the potential to create vigorous and delightful discussions. Some may turn out funny and heartwarming, while others might be unhappy and heartbreaking. But both are special in their own ways.

'So much struggle for this breakfast,' Addya says and laughs. She has gotten up at seven on a Sunday morning to reach here. Everything seems pleasant and optimistic when they enter Taj Mahal Palace Hotel for breakfast. It has a phenomenal location, right opposite the Gateway of India, and the staff treats them like royalty.

'Some of the best conversations happen during a meal,' the mischievous Arjun says while greeting Addya and Tarjani. He emphasizes more on his words when talking to Tarjani, not because she had a rough night but because there is a lot of scope for them to learn something from each other. The three of them settle around the round wooden table and wait for their morning meal to appear.

♥

Enjoying potato whirls from the plate and sipping coffee, Arjun continues the conversation, 'Dimpy Aunty had once said something during my struggling days when I was writing books and was fighting depression and anxiety. She told me that the time has changed now, you must shout out your feelings—about your work, and your life. This is how the world is. And if you are waiting for your helmsman to help you cross the sea of worries and broken heart, your wait will never end. So, always be your own helmsman and do not become dependent on others for your happiness.'

'That's absolutely correct,' Anushka takes long sips of coffee and agrees, not because her mother has said that, but because she believes in it too. Others nod.

'I know it's heavy, with the light breakfast,' she adds.

'But yeah, I completely agree with you,' Tarjani says and Addya gives a thumbs-up.

'So, how did you manage to create such a magnificent piece of artwork that Vivanta by Taj decided to trust you with the entire assignment? It's amazing,' with a booming voice, Arjun says this aloud so that some hotel officials listen to them.

Surprised, Tarjani and Addya look at Arjun because this is something that he has already congratulated Tarjani for. Addya and Tarjani now want more work, not just keep enjoying the work that will cease to exist in the upcoming weeks.

'Yeah...' Tarjani says.

A little louder, he says, 'It's really great that Vivanta by Taj has signed you on.'

This time, they grab the attention of a person from the desk. Arjun continues, 'Why do you not contact this branch of Taj? You can install and showcase your work here.'

Now Tarjani understands what Arjun is trying to do. Insecurities exist everywhere, and hotels are no different in this aspect. Arjun prepares to approach the desk and ask about the right person to talk about the business development.

'Wait, she'll take over,' Tarjani smiles and tells Addya to approach the desk instead.

'That will be wonderful,' Arjun cheers Addya.

'Me?' Addya wonders.

'Yes, c'mon. Go ahead,' they say in unison.

'Hi, who is the manager here?' Addya asks, pretending to look serious and intimidating. Your words define your identity, your tone reveals your authority. Addya holds both at the moment.

'Yes, ma'am, please tell me, how can I help you?' the man at the counter asks her politely. It is the same man who was listening to them.

'I am from Uzaro, we curate antiques and new art pieces as well. I wish to meet the manager,' she asks professionally. Arjun is proud of her and is pleased to see her confidence.

'She is fearless,' murmurs Tarjani. She is happy to have her in her company. There have been many times when Addya has come up with ideas to help Tarjani evolve and expand her wings. What else does an entrepreneur need?

'Sure, ma'am, it will be our pleasure. Would you like to meet Mr Rathore? He is the head in-charge of this facility. I would connect you to him but I am not sure if he is here right now. But please have a seat while I check and get back to you, else you can leave your number here and I will share it with him,' he looks at her.

'That works. Thank you! In case Mr Rathore is around, please let us know, we are here for some more time,' Addya responds and passes her card to that person.

♥

'By the way, I forgot to tell you that we have an event in Dubai on 18 April, and Addya is going to talk about Uzaro and her journey with it,' Tarjani surprises her when she returns.

This is an unbelievable moment for Addya.

'What? I am trying things right now. I haven't cracked anything yet.'

'But you have done well, and you should come with me. I will ask Agastya too if his schedule is free. Many creative people are coming from various fields. There will be painters, singers, musicians…' looking at Arjun, she adds, '…and writers.'

'Seriously? You are also going?' Addya asks Arjun, and adds, 'In that case, I am definitely joining you,' Addya happily agrees.

'Yeah, I got the invitation, but I feel nervous this time,' Arjun says with a wide smile. 'I have a few things to wrap up here, so, I am not sure. But I wish you good luck. You should definitely go.'

Suddenly, Addya notices the call flashing on her screen. Her smile fades away when she sees the number. It is her lawyer—Mr Bhardwaj.

♥

'Hello Uncle,' Addya says, answering his call.

'Good Morning, Addya. I had submitted the document you shared and appealed to transfer your case to Mumbai, but the case cannot be transferred until Delhi Sessions Court surrenders the case, which means they will have to write that they are incapable of solving the case and only then can you proceed further.'

'But they aren't solving the case anyway. All they do is adjourn it to the next date.'

'I understand. But our only solution is to take the case back from the Delhi Sessions Court, which makes the case null and void, and then start from scratch in Bombay Sessions Court. But I'll not suggest that because it will leave a negative impression,' he says sternly.

Lawyers are like doctors, they do not like getting involved in the emotional aspect of their cases so that they can do their job with utmost professionalism. He tells her that he has tried his best and it is up to her to decide the next step.

'I was trying to distract myself and I got a work permit here as well. I am also calling my mother here in a few weeks. If I come to Delhi, I can imagine my life,' Addya gets emotional and tries to find an extreme corner to discuss this without breaking down.

'I know. All your reasons are justified. Everything is correct. But we have laws and we can only stick to those laws. It is about arguments, logics and evidences. There is no value for emotions in court, so we must stay strong and fight. Do you understand me?' he says.

It is ironical—we use logic and proof to fight for emotional issues. That is the law.

Addya pauses and then responds, 'I'll call you after

discussing it with Agastya.'

'No hurry. Take your time and tell Agastya to call me as soon as he can.'

The call disconnects.

'Is everything all right?' Anushka asks her when she returns to her seat, trying to calm the baby she is holding.

'The court has rejected my appeal to transfer the case…'

'But you have proof now, you submitted the documents,' says Anushka.

'Should I talk to the lawyer once again if he can do anything?' Arjun knows this is unfair.

'I have already asked him about all my options,' Addya says and prepares herself mentally to be present in the court for the next date in Delhi.

Twenty-four

*T*his is the ninth date in seven months for her, fighting in multiple cases she has filed to seek justice. They are upset yet hopeful that the court will stand with the righteous and not remain blindfolded.

'Case number 122,' the man announces.

Both the lawyers stand up and take permission to proceed.

'Your Honour, I would like to bring to your kind attention that it is not true that the CCTV cameras were installed only for her. It was a mere coincidence that they were installed before the wedding. We have a witness—the person who installed it. I would like to call him,' says Mr Rastogi.

'Permission granted,' the judge says.

'Is it true that you went to their house and installed it?' Mr Rastogi asks the witness.

'Y...yes I did,' the young man hesitates.

'That's it, Your Honour. Hence, all the allegations against my client Mr Bali and his family are invalid. Thank you,' the lawyer returns to his seat.

'Objection, My Lord!' says Mr Bhardwaj.

'I have some questions for Mr...,' he asks.

'Permission granted,' the judge says.

'Atif Mohammad,' the witness tells him his name. Agastya

looks at him with rage in his eyes.

'Do you have any proof to show when you installed the cameras?' Mr Bhardwaj questions him.

'Sir, I can get it but kindly grant me some time,' he states as if he is prepared what he has to speak.

'Okay, thank you.'

The man nods and goes back to his chair.

'Please give us some time, Your Honour, I have some evidence to share in the next hearing,' says Mr Rastogi.

'Please keep things ready before you come for the hearing. The court shall not entertain such misdemeanour henceforth,' the judge reprimands him.

Mr Bhardwaj interrupts, 'Your Honour, I have something to bring to your kind notice. Mr Bali and his family had filed an application in August 2017 that Mrs Addya escaped their home, but I want to highlight that Mr Bali had gone out of town with Addya in January 2018. That means, the application is invalid, and it was filed without any knowledge and consent of my client. Here is the evidence—the pictures which were clicked. I must add that Mr Bali tried to get rid of them but forgot to remove them from Addya's cellphone, which have the original date and time on them.'

The lawyer presents the photographs to the judge.

He continues, 'Also, Mr Bali and his father simply filed the application for Addya leaving home, even though she hadn't. She was unaware of this act and she was tortured brutally by Mr Bali. He filed a case for divorce to get married to someone else, without her knowledge. Everything was happening right there in front of her and they forced her to run because, on paper, Addya had already left home. That is how deceptive Mr Bali and his family members are. That's it.'

'Can you provide some relevant proofs apart from these pictures? The date and time on the pictures cannot always be verified,' the judge looks at all the pictures and hands them over to his stenographer who keeps them in the drawer.

'But...' before Mr Bhardwaj can say anything, Mr Rastogi pitches in, 'Your Honour, this is irrelevant information. Moreover, I have something else to share regarding the case. Mrs Addya had started her career with Indian Airlines, and she was fired from her very first job with immediate effect. The reason was that she was drunk on duty. Here are the documents.' The lawyer presents the report to the court.

Everyone looks at Addya and things change dramatically. Impatiently, Addya stands up in her place and shouts, 'Sir, that is not related to this case.'

'Please respect the decorum of the court and whatever you want to say, speak here,' the judge announces and points to the stand.

Agastya and his lawyer did not know about this and are afraid of how it will be represented; they look unsettled.

'Sir, this case is not related to my past work experience,' she states.

'It is important because that speaks volumes about her personality and character...'

Before the plaintiff's lawyer completes his words, Mr Bhardwaj interrupts, 'You do not need to talk about her character here.' And he continues, 'Your Honour, he is trying to mislead the court. I need to discuss this with my client and we need some time.'

'Proceed.'

Hopelessly, he closes his file and waits for the judge to announce the next date.

'Next date—18 April.' The judge hits the gavel. Agastya looks for Atif Mohammad before he takes Addya home.

♥

Addya feels like she is trapped in a dark hole. She should have told her lawyer these things when he had asked everything about her life. She knows it will weaken her case now. She feels like she is drowning.

In the worst time of her life, petty things that never mattered in the past matter more than the present. She forgot that burns always leave their mark. So does our past—a deep scar.

♥

Everyone has a past. We all have stories we never wish to share with anyone. Addya did not know that her stories would become a baggage in her future. Addya closes the door of her room and lies down on her bed, pretending to be unwell. She is not afraid of answering Agastya or her mother's questions, she just does not wish to talk about anything at the moment.

Agastya knocks on the door three times and opens it. Addya leans against the bed and Agastya sits on the bed. 'Why did you hide this from the whole family? You didn't even share it with me?' he asks her. Agastya does not know how to come out of what has happened in the court today. Whenever things seem to settle and stabilize, something crops up. Addya feels helpless and regrets hiding this from Agastya.

Addya had joined Indian Airlines after she had graduated

because she wanted to join the aviation industry. Though her family had been reluctant, being the oldest in the family, she had convinced them and had started her training in Delhi. Everything had been going fine when one day she had been out with her friends on her birthday and her friends had forced her to drink. Next day, she had a breath analyzer test before boarding a flight. In the test, 0.01 per cent alcohol was detected and she had been suspended for three months. So, she had resigned and had joined another airline to give herself a fresh start. She had taken a pragmatic step that had seemed the best thing to do at that time, so she never told her family about this incident. But she had never wanted to hide anything from the person she was married to. So, she had shared it with Bali and this is what it had resulted into—she had received misery for her honesty.

Addya shares this with Agastya.

'Addya! It's okay,' Agastya says, no longer frustrated after listening to the real story. However, he is still worried about what had happened in court and how it had impacted their mother.

'But I was not fired, I was suspended, and it's written in the letter,' Addya says and remembers the time when everyone had judged her after the breath analyzer test. It had flashed before her eyes when the lawyer had recounted it in the court to malign her character.

'It's written that you were found indulging in alcohol on duty. Do you think that makes the situation easier?' Agastya tries to reason with her. He cannot think of a solution. He wonders how the smallest decisions can make such huge impacts in life.

He adds, 'I always tell you that if you are suffering, speak out or call a doctor or a therapist. You cannot simply believe that you can resolve everything. Getting help for mental health is as important as calling the police after a murder.' Agastya looks into her eyes and continues, 'So, help yourself before someone else picks on you—before it is too late.'

'I don't know what others would do in this kind of a situation,' Addya says and then turns silent.

'Well, you sleep, let's see what we can do,' Agastya gets up, covers the baby with the blanket and switches off the lights. The door closes.

Reaching for the bedside lamp, she stops and withdraws her hand. The photograph of her father is facing the room. She stands there every night before she goes to sleep. It has always faced her, not away from her. Addya fights her tears but feels a growing lump in her throat and a painful sting in her eyes. Everything around her becomes irrelevant. Staring at the reflection in the mirror across the bed, she falls asleep.

Twenty-five

Agastya is weary. When after some time he cannot bear it, he calls the lawyer early morning. Even in anger, he has a sense of pleading in his voice. He says, 'Uncle why are you not able to solve the case? We are not even able to defend the case. We are just getting dates. My sister needs a divorce but with all the rights she deserves. That man took all her savings, treated her like an animal every day. Don't they see marks on her skin? Is it that tough to get justice?'

'Yes, Agastya, it is that tough to get justice. Marks can be created, and people do that, so the only way is to come up with proof, which we do not have as of now. And even if we do, they are not substantial enough to steer in our favour. We need to sit and discuss in detail. This is becoming complex, but we are trying,' the lawyer says.

'Okay. I will see you tomorrow.'

♥

'Life has betrayed me at every point in life; I'm fed up with this world. I want to take the case back. I was only fighting for my rights and respect that I am already losing in the process of attaining justice. I am just regretting my decision.

I would rather leave this country and settle somewhere far off where respect and dignity actually exist, than have myself condemned for fighting the societal atrocities,' an exhausted Addya says in fury.

Agastya looks at her—the penetrating stare makes her regret being so negative.

'Nothing has deluded you. Do not judge your whole life just because things are not in your favour. Let me tell you one thing, you are just thirty and still have a long life to live. I promise you that I will give you what you have lost, even more than that. I just want you to stay strong.'

Agastya holds her shoulders and looks into her regretful eyes, which are now filled with strength. This reminds her of her childhood when her father used to teach her life lessons holding both her shoulders to make her feel strong. It worked then, but it does not work now.

'It's easy to say but how do we prove that in the court. No one knows about my situation. The court thinks he never hit me. He used to grab my neck so tightly that it was sore for days. He would leave cigarette marks on my skin and would give me shocks with the gas lighter when I dared to say, "Not tonight." How can I make them believe that all this happened to me, and not just once, but many times,' Addya says, in tears.

Agastya remains silent. A new bout of rage appears in his eyes. A passive aggressive muffled rage. He restrains his thoughts and says, 'Once you think negatively, you start feeling worse. And then it sticks. It lingers. It is always there. Always. So, do whatever you feel like, just do not let negativity enter your life. You have to be the strongest right now, for mom and for me, even if it goes beyond this. We'll fight until you get what you deserve.'

Agastya controls his tears and Addya hugs him tightly. Her grip is enough to define her emotions. She cries, 'I want to do something so that I can change my life to how it was before. I want to come out of this. It eats me day and night.'

Nothing can break Agastya but tears in his sister's eyes shatter him into pieces. 'I know. I will take you out of this. I can get back everything you had before, trust me.'

A message from Tarjani flashes on his cellphone.

> Why is Addya not picking up my calls? Where are you? Is everything okay?

Agastya replies.

> All ok. I'll call you back.

He takes the water bottle and gives it to Addya.

'Tarjani told me that you are going for the event in Dubai. She trusts your work and understands your skills. You can also help her in e-commerce organization and brand building. You are now an important part of Uzaro and are going to Dubai—that's no mean feat. Very few people get a chance to speak at such an esteemed platform. So, for now, please try to concentrate on that,' Agastya says, looking at her.

She wants to implement his words. She continues, 'I don't know... I know I can't change the things that have happened in the past but at least I'll not have regrets in life that I did not try, right?' She looks for his suggestions and strength as she is unsure.

Agastya thinks about something for a moment and then says, 'That's why I was telling you to concentrate on things which inspire and give you joy. You both have done some commendable work together. Trust me, even I didn't think when I saw Uzaro for the first time that it would attain global recognition. She has made it that big single-handedly. If she thinks you can be of help and you both can take it forward, what is stopping you? You should definitely take it up.'

'But I am worried, can the date be changed? Because I guess the event is on the same date—April 18.'

Agastya pauses and says, 'I'll talk to the lawyer. I am sure the date can be postponed. So, let us keep everything aside and you prepare your speech. Once you come back, we'll talk about the case, okay?' he beams.

'There is no "you", you are also coming with me. Tarjani won't be able to join us because she has to take care of a few deals she has recently secured from a restaurant chain, but she discussed it with Arjun and Dimpy Aunty, and Dimpy Aunty is also coming with us. So, you must too. Arjun said he'll talk to you about your flight tickets.' Now that Addya knows she will be with the people she loves most, she is looking forward to travelling with them.

'Oh yes, I do not have the luxury of international sponsored travel,' Agastya mocks her.

'Just like the rest of the year when you roam around sponsored,' Addya responds cheekily.

'Let me talk to Arjun and Dimpy Aunty and discuss the plan,' Agastya says and leaves the room.

Agastya also wants Tarjani to join them. He thinks of calling Tarjani, but first he needs to call the lawyer.

♥

Agastya knows how excited Addya is about the event and he is even more excited to see her fall back in love with life. He has to speak to Mr Bhardwaj about the possibilities of postponing the date because if Addya is not present at the hearing, it will weaken her case and Mr Rastogi will appeal for ex parte. An ex parte decision is one that is decided by the judge in the absence of the other, which means Addya will lose the case.

'The court has given the final date and you should bring Addya,' says the lawyer. Agastya pauses.

'Nothing can be done?' he asks him again.

'I can try but if the application gets rejected, it will be a problem. If we could avoid the appeal we filed before to transfer the case outside Delhi, there would be a chance to postpone the date easily, but for now, I suggest that you be available for 18 April. We are leaving a bad impression on the judiciary from the very first notice because we never received two notices, and only appeared in court after the third one. We are on the right side, but I hope you understand the situation.'

'Okay. Thank you,' says Agastya and disconnects the call. This is when Addya enters Agastya's room.

♥

Asking questions does not mean doubting someone. They are meant to be asked to get answers and then move on. No matter how strong your bond with the person is, when you have a question you should ask before it becomes a dilemma. Addya had often noticed Agastya talking over the phone in a hushed voice with someone but she ignored it. However, today, she had found a new cellphone in his drawer when looking for her credit card.

Addya casually asks Agastya, 'Whose phone is this?'

His expressions create confusion, he takes the cellphone from her hand, and switches it off.

'Nothing, it's an official phone,' he says.

'This? Was there nothing older than this?' she says while looking at the cellphone. Addya suspects that Agastya is not telling her everything.

'Are you hiding something?' she questions. Expressions matter as much as words. Agastya gets conscious and responds, 'Are you doubting me?'

'Never. I trust you.'

'Then don't worry about things. Also, I spoke to the lawyer, and the date will be postponed. So, you can happily go ahead and deliver your best speech. But make sure you prepare a good one. Let me know if you need any help. Tarjani suggested we go to Mumbai, and then we will all go together to Dubai. She has booked our tickets accordingly,' Agastya pinches her chin and goes back to his work.

Twenty-six

A week later, at 9.00 in the morning, everyone waits at Gate no. 39C to board their flight from Mumbai to Dubai. While Arjun and Dimpy Aunty are busy clicking selfies, Addya receives a message on her cellphone. It is from Tarjani.

All the best.
I'm excited to watch your speech on a video call.

Thanks a ton.
Don't make me nervous :)

You will do great. I know.
Gotta go. I need to get ready for a meeting. See you!

See you!

Addya comes and sits next to Agastya, 'You know, when we love someone, we do it without any reason, but we always meet that person for some purpose. Some people enter our lives to shape it beautifully, and I must say, Tarjani has come to ours for the same reason. I used to feel hopeless and frustrated every time I woke up in the morning, wishing I could end my pain and sleep forever. However, every time I sought help, she was there. It may sound dramatic, but she has been an epitome of support and selfless love.'

'Are you trying to revise your speech with me?' Agastya pulls her legs.

Addya punches him playfully, 'I am serious. You should meet her mother. By the way, did the lawyer confirm the date for the next hearing?'

'He will share the next date some time today or tomorrow, but we are not going to discuss this further. We mutually decided that, right?'

'Okay. Okay,' says Addya.

'And I will make sure you have a good life ahead,' says Agastya and looks at the cellphone that Addya had enquired about a few days ago. He types something and takes the newspaper that he had picked from the Delhi airport out from his bag. It is a Delhi edition. He opens and reads the local news—a man died in an accident last night. Agastya almost squeezes the newspaper, takes the cellphone, removes its SIM card, gets up and throws it in the bin.

'What happened?' Addya enquires.

Agastya looks at Addya and simply says, 'Nothing important.'

He smiles nervously and calls everyone as the gate opens to board the flight.

♥

'Where are you going?' Arjun asks Addya.

'Why to take a chance?' an excited and nervous Addya stands up and plans to use the restroom moments before going on stage.

'Did Dimpy Aunty ask you to do this?' he looks at Dimpy Aunty with a raised brow. She ignores him, saying, 'You do not have a copyright on that act.'

'Be cool and just chill,' Arjun smiles and makes her comfortable, 'A-D-D-Y-A...' he holds her hand and squeezes it.

'Being nervous is obvious but don't pretend that you're too open. Be decent but don't flatter,' Arjun says when he returns.

'Are you repeating her words?' Addya looks at Dimpy Aunty.

'He has been doing that for years,' she laughs.

♥

'Please welcome Addya on stage,' the gorgeous woman on the stage calls Addya. She looks flawless, and she is exuding confidence and charm tonight. She carries herself gracefully to the stage. All her hardships pay off today. Once on the stage, Addya greets everyone and receives a massive round of applause. She commences without much ado.

'Hi everyone! Today I am not going to talk about how much revenue we have generated so far, how many satisfied clients we hold or how much debt we are in.'

She hears some giggles in the crowd.

She continues, 'I am going to talk about our beliefs as a brand, which is in line with real life and hopefully all of you will be able to relate and learn from it. I joined the Uzaro team a few months ago, and it was nothing like getting a job in the normal way people do. Well, I was actually stuck in my personal life due to a bad marriage, and in fact, I am currently fighting a case to get justice for my child and myself. During these tough times, one thing that came like a rainbow in my life was an offer to be a part of Uzaro. I will tell you why I describe Uzaro in my life as a "rainbow".

'I was stuck, depressed and taking sleeping pills because I felt life had not been fair to me. A lousy marriage was acting like slow poison. But when Uzaro happened, my directionless life got a new direction, thanks to team Uzaro and Tarjani, well if you do not know, she is the founder of Uzaro. Uzaro is one brand that holds true to its meaning, which is, tiny smiles. At every small and big win, we thank our clients and our internal teams so that we grow and build good relationships at the same time.

'I would like to highlight that this year we got 68 per cent of our work from references through existing clients or friends and family. We create unique artwork using broken things. This resembles real life—no matter how broken one is, one has the potential to shine. But we have to believe and take action, otherwise—yes, we remain broken.

'Fixing is not an easy job, and creating something new is even tougher. But Tarjani always believes and practises simple formulas—the first one being, "Build relationships because word of mouth is the best possible marketing". It is less expensive and more impactful.

'On this note, I would like to share a famous Sanskrit slokas, first, *"Mum Niyatim Niychami"*, which means one controls his/her own destiny. So, give your heart a break from negative thoughts, worries, false assumptions and walk on a positive path. Spread smiles, be different, and in no time, you will shine because you will be able to control your destiny through righteous actions.

'And the second is *"Na Kadapi Khandhit"* which means

never broken. So, we create unique art products using broken things which have the potential to grow and shine with their inherent light. Thank you.'

Addya joins her hands, bows to the audience and leaves the stage amidst applause. Everyone claps. Tarjani is tearful over the video call when she sees Addya alight the stage. She feels proud that Addya has represented Uzaro with such grace. Arjun and Dimpy Aunty step forward and give her a warm hug.

Agastya is choking with emotions seeing his strong sister now, so different from what she had been a few months ago. Tears roll down his cheeks. They all head out.

♥

Arjun rushes towards Agastya and questions him, 'Where is your cellphone?'

'It's switched off,' responds Agastya.

'What happened?' asks Addya.

'I got a call from your home. Bali met with an accident last night. He died.'

'Okay,' says Agastya. Arjun keeps staring at Agastya, surprised at the lack of expression on his face. Agastya avoids eye contact with Addya because if they meet, they may reveal the truth. Addya looks away, wipes a teardrop, and continues to walk towards the exit, which is going to open a new door for her. We all have stories and it is not important how complex your story seems, but how simply it ends. Agastya ends hers today.

Twenty-seven

Both the lawyers stand up and take permission to proceed.

'I want to ask a few questions. Do I have the permission, My Lord?' Mr Rastogi asks.

'Permission granted.'

Mr Rastogi calls Agastya to the stand.

'Well, let me ask you this. Where were you that day Mr Bali was found dead in a car accident?'

'I was travelling to Dubai with my sister, Addya. I believe the documents have been submitted for verification,' replies Agastya.

The judge looks at the boarding pass and documents, with the date and time written on it.

'Did you threaten Bali and his parents seven months ago?'

'Yes, I did, and any brother whose sister has suffered, thus would do the same.'

The judge looks at Mr Bhardwaj. 'Mr Bhardwaj, would you like to cross-examine?'

'No, Your Honour.'

The plaintiff's lawyer proceeds, 'Why did you take Addya to a new city, Mumbai, when her hearings were being conducted here?'

'Yes, sir. I did. She is my sister, and she was getting threat calls here, so for her safety, we relocated to Mumbai for some days,' Agastya responds calmly.

Mr Bhardwaj rises immediately, 'Also, I would like to bring to your notice, My Lord, that these threat calls were reported to a lady police officer, and she said that it was normal, and that she herself receives such calls. She asked us to ignore these calls. In such a scenario, relocating was the only solution my client had. Nothing else.'

'When did you come to know about Mr Bali's death?' Mr Rastogi continues.

'When we were in Dubai. The news reached us the next day in the evening.'

'My Lord, I object. There is no evidence that proves my client guilty. Mr Rastogi is wasting the court's time by asking invalid questions,' Mr Bhardwaj interrupts.

Mr Rastogi requests, 'I would like to request for another date.'

'Order! Order! I would request both the lawyers to settle down and maintain the decorum of the court. I will hear the arguments of both the sides in the next hearing. Till then, the court is adjourned.'

The judge hits the gavel. Next date—20 June.

Exhausted with the growing conflicts, Agastya reaches out for his phone. He opens the video footage in which Bali grabs Addya's neck, suffocating her, and then his father threatens her with the wire, broom and the knife lying in the balcony. With rage coursing through his veins, he sends the video to Bali's father.

♥

On receiving the video, Bali's father's hands tremble as he gasps heavily, clutching the phone tightly. His eyes turn red when he thinks about his past deeds and and he tries to recall Agastya talking to Atif Mohammad after the session in the court. He can't breathe—it feels like someone is choking him.

Mr Rastogi is sitting in front of him on the sofa. Looking at his condition, he asks, 'What happened?'

'I want to withdraw the case.'

'You can withdraw your case, but you'll have to fight the ones that Addya has filed against you,' says Mr Rastogi.

'Can you talk to her lawyer. Please request the court and tell them that I am ready to compromise. She can take whatever she wants.'

Mr Rastogi says, 'It seems the problem is that she doesn't want anything from you now.'

Present Day

Epilogue

A time comes when you try hard to fix things in life and then there comes a time when everything breaks leaving you hopeless and dejected—broken, broken beyond repair. That moment, you feel free because you have nothing to fix and have to start afresh. Only when you come out of your vulnerable zone do you realize that life is worth living. One must simply hold on and stay strong while experiencing a transition from rainstorm to sunshine.

With the sun casting a warm glow, Addya and Agastya feel something new. Sitting together, watching Takshika play in the garden, it feels as if invisible holes were drilled in her skin during the night and all her tension was sucked out. Her steps feel lighter and she tilts her face towards the brilliant streaks of the sun, breaking through her long hair. This is what happens when a battle is over—the battle of life that Addya has won.

She, now, helps others combat depression and anxiety, that many of us go through at least once in our lifetime. She counsels people to focus on themselves, acknowledge their depression and fight the demons within. Whatever spare time she gets, she ensures that she is making herself the priority. She relishes this time and pampers herself unabashedly. Settled in Delhi, today, she is a thankful sister and a part of Uzaro—the tiny smiles.

Here are a bunch of lovely people sharing their feelings.

Dimpy Aunty: I don't have a son, so my world revolves around Arjun. I have given him the right to ask me for anything and discuss things that he cannot even discuss with his mother. I know she gets a bit jealous at times, but that is inevitable. And that's our bond. Our pride.

Agastya: I know that love is a painful venture. My love for Addya is unconditional, but Tarjani is the missing piece of the puzzle to my heart. She made me realize that a man can love two women because love does not divide, it only multiplies with time. At one point of time, I wanted to end things with her, and that night, I cried the most in my life. But when she gave up on her work just to see me, that was the moment I decided that I am not letting her go. Not this time.

Tarjani: Initially, I disliked Addya. It was difficult to accept her growing dependence on Agastya because he was unable to give me the time I deserved. But when I spent more time with Addya, Arjun, and Dimpy Aunty in particular, my perspective changed. They have become an essential part of my life now. Good people bring out the goodness in others.

Holding onto them is the key to achieve happiness.

Addya: I am lucky to have brothers like Arjun and Agastya. I have nothing else to say.

Arjun: I do not know, but every time I finish my book, I cry for a while and then send my first draft to the editor. For this book, we have shed tears for more than a year for Addya, but I'm glad that people know me by her name. It is a moment of pride that I shall always cherish.

A note from the author

Whether I shall turn out to be the hero of my own life or not, these pages will reveal. I do not know how it happens, but every time I start writing a new book, I aspire to pen down content that my readers can relate to, and find a joyous escape in—one that will motivate them to fight the odds in life.

So, if you don't trust the author, that is okay; but you can certainly believe the woman who said this to me a few years ago. The one who inspired me to accept my imperfections and helped me overcome my depression, to be the man I endeavoured to be one day. She is Dimpy Aunty. The one who pokes her nose in everything, right from my personal to professional life, one who radiates positivity, one who is sitting next to me right now, giving me lessons on body-building, trying to flex her non-existent muscles, while I look at her, amused. While I pen down these words, it all seems worth the trouble. She is an essential part of me.

I took time to look around for inspiration and then Dimpy Aunty forced me to write about my own family. This book is an aftermath of her persuasion. It is a risky venture when you have to come out and speak about your own family, but if I don't, then who will? So, I write your stories, for you.

It was painful and heart-wrenching to write a story about

my sister's life. At times, I wondered if I was being a cruel monster, causing people to spill tears over the stories that I write. Maybe... But it's so much more than that. Emotions are a beautiful part of what makes us human, both the good and the bad ones. They are a part of who we are. We should accept them.

The unhappy days in our life make the happy ones brighter, and we have all had days when it just feels right to be in despair. It is hard to explain, but there is a beauty in sorrow too—the beauty that enriches us to appreciate the good times.

My protagonists do not always succeed. They often get hurt, because they are not fictitious. They are either 'you' or 'me', and neither of us are superheroes in real life. We do not win every battle; but we fight, and we fight till the end. We fight to survive. No matter how many times we fall and are torn apart, we get up and fight. That is how life should be lived. So, it is okay if you are going through something which is bothering you, keep fighting.

They say that behind a successful man, there is a woman, but in my case, there are three who have contributed to my prosperity. It gives me immense pleasure to write about them.

Firstly, I would like to start with my mother who firmly inculcated the right family values in me and directed me to walk on the right path, no matter how hard it seemed. Today, I thank her for taking all the important decisions on my behalf. I can never forget her words of wisdom that helped me survive the early days of college and they still inspire me to fight my daily battles. She said, 'Life is on an incline, either you go up or you go down; there is no place to be stagnant', and the second thing she said, which I still follow, is 'Life teaches you everything that you don't wish to, but you have to learn from it, anyway.'

The second person is the first girl who came into my life when I had just begun to understand the meaning of love. She made me experience the different realms of love, some good, and some bad. She left me for no reason, and made me feel that I was good for nothing. I do not want to forget her. She taught me things nobody else could.

The final name I would like to mention with tremendous pride is Anushka's, who came into my life along with Dimpy Aunty and held me strong until I realized the worth of my existence after six months of gruelling depression. It was the most trying phase of my life. Though she made me work very hard with my emotions to get the best out of me, it all seems worth the hassle. Thank you to these wonderful women for transforming my life. Trust me, it's worth being with you, and I mean it. Also, thank you for making my life easier by going through the edits.

A special mention to my father, my mentor, Mr Ashok Tiwari, who has always inspired me to work hard, and strive with undying enthusiasm. It would be impossible for me to take ownership of the multiple roles I play without mentioning him. My unconditional love to Neeraj for loving and understanding me.

Thanks to Shreya, Gaurang, Harsh and Rahul Mohandas. And my heartfelt and genuine gratitude to all with whom I am connected.

And lastly—I intentionally write about my readers at the end so that I can end the book with my appreciation for them— you have always been my strength. Thank you for making me who I am today. It is your love and blessing that encourages me to write true stories that hold the potential to inspire us. You all mean a lot to me. Stay connected. Keep smiling. See you someday, somewhere, sometime.